# Build Your Vocabulary 2

## John Flower

with

**Michael Berman**
and
**Mark Powell**

LTP
LANGUAGE

**LANGUAGE TEACHING PUBLICATIONS**
**35 Church Road, Hove, BN3 2BE, England**

ISBN 0 906717 77 9
© LTP 1989
New Edition 1995

**The Author**
John Flower is a teacher at Eurocentre Bournemouth where he has
worked for many years. He has long experience of teaching students at
all levels and has prepared many students for the Cambridge
examinations. He is the author of First Certificate Organiser, Phrasal
Verb Organiser, and Build Your Business Vocabulary.

**Personal Note**
The author would like to express his thanks to Michael Lewis for his
enthusiasm and guidance, to Michael Berman who contributed some
lively ideas for alternative ways to build vocabulary, and to Mark Powell
for some more lexical exercises for this new edition. He would also like to
thank his colleagues and students for their help, his wife for her typing
and advice, and his children for not making too much noise!

**Acknowledgements**
Cover Design by Anna Macleod.
Illustrations by James Slater.
Ideas for illustrations from Argos.
Printed in England by Commercial Colour Press, London E7.

# Contents

# Read this before you start

So you plan to build your vocabulary! Learning vocabulary is a very important part of learning English. If you make a grammar mistake, it may be "wrong" but very often people will understand you anyway. But if you don't know the exact word that you need, it is very frustrating for you, and the person you are talking to. Good English means having a big vocabulary!

There are better and worse ways to build your vocabulary and this book will help you to build your vocabulary quickly and effectively.
You will find it is best to work:

● systematically
● regularly
● personally

Don't just make lists of all the new words you meet — plan and choose. Think of areas **you** are interested in; look for things **you** can't say in English, then fill those gaps in **your** vocabulary.

Don't do ten pages one day then nothing for three weeks! Try to do one or two pages every day. Regular work will help you to build effectively.

Don't just learn words; you also need to know how to use them. Which words does a word often combine with? This book will help you to learn more words, but also how to use the words you know more effectively. That is an important part of building your vocabulary.

Don't just use your dictionary when you have a problem. It is an important resource. It can help you in lots of different ways. There are tips all through this book to help you use your dictionary effectively.

Don't just make lists of new words; organise them. Again, there are tips to help you to learn and remember more of what you study.

Finally, there are a lot of words in English. Building your vocabulary is a long job! There are two more books in this series to help you learn more words, and to help you to enjoy the job!

# 1 Using a dictionary

If you want to learn English vocabulary, you should have a good English-English dictionary.

Use one with explanations that are easy to understand and which has sentences showing how you use the words.

Practise using a dictionary by answering these questions.

## 1. Meaning

Which one of these is part of a flower?

**paddle**          **pedal**          **pension**          **petal**          **puddle**

Of course a dictionary gives you a definition, but it helps you in other ways too. The next questions show you how.

## 2. Words which go together

Match a verb on the left with a noun on the right.
Use each word once only.

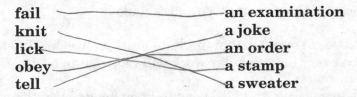

| | |
|---|---|
| fail | an examination |
| knit | a joke |
| lick | an order |
| obey | a stamp |
| tell | a sweater |

Some words often occur with other words; they form word partnerships. A good dictionary will give examples of the way in which words go together like this.

## 3. Phrasal verbs

Complete each sentence by using the correct word.
He looked the word . . . . . . . . . . in a dictionary.
Look . . . . . . . . . .! There's a car coming!
His nurse looks . . . . . . . . . . him very well.
Are you still looking . . . . . . . . . . that book you lost?

Phrasal verbs are another example of words going together. Look up some common verbs in English and see what examples you can find.

# 4. Word formation

Use the correct form of the word ORIGIN in each sentence.

The teacher said his writing showed . . . . . . . . .
I think your . . . . . . . . plan was the best one.
They . . . . . . . . wanted to stay for two weeks.

> Words often have different grammatical forms. A good dictionary will show you these.

# 5. Pronunciation

Which of these words has a different vowel sound?

| | | | |
|---|---|---|---|
| knew | sew | few | true |
| bought | caught | cough | fort |
| treat | sweat | feet | meet |
| height | weight | late | great |
| most | roast | post | lost |

> You don't really know a word until you know how to pronounce it properly. This is why a good dictionary shows you the pronunciation of each word.
>
> It is not only the sound but the stress pattern which is important, as the next question shows.

# 6. Stress

Underline the part of the word which has the main stress.
Examples: **pho**tograph   pho**tog**rapher

| | | |
|---|---|---|
| complete | origin | pedal |
| correct | original | together |
| dictionary | originality | understand |
| explanation | originally | vocabulary |

> Remember you can use your dictionary in many ways — not just when you are not sure of the meaning of a word!

# 2  Word groups

It is useful to make a list of the words you use when you talk about a subject. When you learn a new word, you can add it to your list.

This book will give you some ideas but why don't you think of some subjects **you** are interested in and see how many words you can think of?

Put each of the words below into the correct list. Use each word once only. Can you think of any more words to add to each list?

| | | | |
|---|---|---|---|
| accelerator | flowers | necklace | score |
| brake | giraffe | plant | single |
| brooch | goal | platform | station |
| dig | hedge | referee | team |
| earring | lion | return | tyre |
| elephant | monkey | ring | windscreen |

**1. ANIMALS**

giraffe
elephant
monkey
lion

**2. THE CAR**

brake
tyre
windscreen
accelerator

**3. FOOTBALL**

score
goal
refree
team

**4. THE GARDEN**

flowers
plant
dig
hedge

**5. JEWELLERY**

brooch
necklace
ring
earring

**6. RAIL TRAVEL**

platform
single
return
station

8

# 3 Everyday conversations – 1

**French food is the best in the world.
— Do you really think so?**

Match each sentence on the left with the best response on the right. Use each response once only.

1.  Could you repeat that, please? (ι)
2.  What do you do?   L
3.  I'm afraid I can't come this evening.  b
4.  How do you do. (a)
5.  Where do you come from? (h)
6.  French food is the best in the world. (j)
7.  I'm afraid I haven't got a pen. (c)
8.  How are you? (k)
9.  I'm taking my driving test tomorrow. (d)
10. Have you got the time, please? (f)
11. I hope the weather will get better. (g)
12. Have a nice time. (e)

a.  How do you do.
b.  Oh dear! What a pity!
c.  Never mind. You can borrow mine.
d.  Good luck!
e.  Thanks. You too.
f.  Yes. It's half past three.
g.  So do I.
h.  Indonesia.
i.  Yes, of course.
j.  Do you really think so?
k.  Fine, thanks — and you?
l.  I'm a journalist.

Write your answers here:

| 1 | 2 | 3 | 4 | 5 | 6 | 7 | 8 | 9 | 10 | 11 | 12 |
|---|---|---|---|---|---|---|---|---|----|----|----|
|   |   |   |   |   |   |   |   |   |    |    |    |

Can you think of any more responses you could give to the sentences on the left?

# 4 Word partnerships – 1

Some pairs of words often occur together. This makes listening and reading easier because when you see one word you expect the other. Here are some partnerships.

Match the verb on the left with a noun on the right. Use each word once only. Write your answers in the boxes.

## Set 1

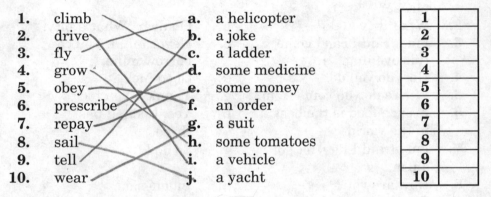

| | | | |
|---|---|---|---|
| 1. | climb | a. | a helicopter |
| 2. | drive | b. | a joke |
| 3. | fly | c. | a ladder |
| 4. | grow | d. | some medicine |
| 5. | obey | e. | some money |
| 6. | prescribe | f. | an order |
| 7. | repay | g. | a suit |
| 8. | sail | h. | some tomatoes |
| 9. | tell | i. | a vehicle |
| 10. | wear | j. | a yacht |

| 1 | |
|---|---|
| 2 | |
| 3 | |
| 4 | |
| 5 | |
| 6 | |
| 7 | |
| 8 | |
| 9 | |
| 10 | |

## Set 2

Now do the same with these words.

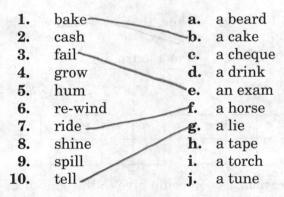

| | | | |
|---|---|---|---|
| 1. | bake | a. | a beard |
| 2. | cash | b. | a cake |
| 3. | fail | c. | a cheque |
| 4. | grow | d. | a drink |
| 5. | hum | e. | an exam |
| 6. | re-wind | f. | a horse |
| 7. | ride | g. | a lie |
| 8. | shine | h. | a tape |
| 9. | spill | i. | a torch |
| 10. | tell | j. | a tune |

| 1 | |
|---|---|
| 2 | |
| 3 | |
| 4 | |
| 5 | |
| 6 | |
| 7 | |
| 8 | |
| 9 | |
| 10 | |

# 5  The department store

Learn English and test your memory by using the world around you.

When you go shopping, ask yourself if you know the English names of the products you see. Do you know the names of the departments in a store where you might find these products? Make a list of the different departments you find in a store and write the names of products you might see in them. The exercise below should give you some ideas.

Below is a plan of a large department store. In which department would you expect to buy each of the following? You should have to go to each department once only.

1.   an armchair
2.   a bar of chocolate
3.   a brooch
4.   a clarinet
5.   a doll
6.   an encyclopedia
7.   some lettuce seeds
8.   some lipstick
9.   a meat pie
10.  a pair of sandals
11.  a pair of sheets
12.  a pair of skis
13.  a rug
14.  a saucepan
15.  a skirt
16.  a tie
17.  some typing paper
18.  a video recorder

| a. FURNITURE | | b. CARPETS | |
|---|---|---|---|
| c. MEN'S WEAR | d. TOYS | e. MUSIC | |
| f. LADIES' WEAR | | g. ELECTRICAL | |
| h. STATIONERY | i. BOOKS | j. COOKWARE | k. SPORTS |
| l. JEWELLERY | m. COSMETICS | n. SHOES  o. CONFECTIONERY | |
| p. HOUSEHOLD LINEN | q. DELICATESSEN | r. GARDENING | |

Write your answers here:

| 1 | 2 | 3 | 4 | 5 | 6 | 7 | 8 | 9 | 10 | 11 | 12 | 13 | 14 | 15 | 16 | 17 | 18 |
|---|---|---|---|---|---|---|---|---|---|---|---|---|---|---|---|---|---|
|   |   |   |   |   |   |   |   |   |    |    |    |    |    |    |    |    |    |

Can you think of any more things you might find in these departments?

# 6   Which person is it?

If you see or hear certain words you can often guess what is being spoken about and predict other words that may occur.

After you have done this exercise, underline any words connected with the answer, for example 'sheep' and 'mountain' in the first sentence.

You don't need to understand **every** word to understand what someone says. Good guessing is important too!

Choose the best word to complete the sentence.
Look up any words you don't know.

1. The . . . . . . . . took his sheep up the mountain.
   **a.** tailor       **b.** florist        **c.** shepherd        **d.** burglar
2. She got a . . . . . . . . to mend the leaking pipe.
   **a.** traitor      **b.** plumber       **c.** accountant      **d.** docker
3. The . . . . . . . . broke into our house while we were away.
   **a.** umpire       **b.** trainee       **c.** politician      **d.** burglar
4. A . . . . . . . . from each branch came to the meeting.
   **a.** dentist      **b.** representative **c.** maid            **d.** hunter
5. Most . . . . . . . . dream of leading their party one day.
   **a.** hosts        **b.** caretakers    **c.** guests          **d.** politicians
6. After he came out of prison, he had to report to his
   . . . . . . . . once a week.
   **a.** referee      **b.** carpenter     **c.** probation officer **d.** chef
7. The . . . . . . . . said my sign meant I was very romantic.
   **a.** astrologer   **b.** astronomer    **c.** applicant       **d.** diplomat
8. I asked the . . . . . . . . to make the sleeves a bit shorter.
   **a.** sailor       **b.** tailor        **c.** carpenter       **d.** courier
9. It took the . . . . . . . . three hours to unload the ship.
   **a.** dockers      **b.** auctioneers   **c.** undertakers     **d.** miners
10. All . . . . . . . . for the job must fill in the correct form.
    **a.** brides      **b.** employers     **c.** employees       **d.** applicants
11. Shop assistants never like serving difficult . . . . . . . . . . .
    **a.** guests      **b.** consumers     **c.** customers       **d.** clients
12. The . . . . . . . . welcomed them to his church.
    **a.** psychiatrist **b.** priest       **c.** stunt man       **d.** optician

# 7   Memory game

Can you name all the things in the picture? Use each of these words once only:

| | | | |
|---|---|---|---|
| alarm clock | comb | lighter | suitcase |
| ambulance | corkscrew | newspaper | teddy bear |
| banana | cup and saucer | parcel | toothbrush |
| camera | dollar bill | postcard | top hat |
| cassette | key | shoe | train |

1. ...top hat..   2. ...train..   3. ...teddy bear..   4. ....comb...

5. ..cassette..   6. ..dollar bill..   7. cup..and saucer   8. ..newspaper

9. ....postcard   10. ...suitcase..   11. alarm clock..   12. ...camera

13. ..banana..   14. ..toothbrush..   15. ambulance   16. ...lighter..

17. .....key...   18. ...parcel..   19. ...shoe...   20. corkscrew

Later in the book, you will be asked how many of these words you can remember — without looking at the words again!

# 8 'Come' and 'get'

Many words in English can be used in different ways.

When you look up a word in a dictionary, don't stop at the first definition. See how many other ways you can use it. Sometimes one meaning is similar to another; sometimes the same word has several completely different meanings.

Don't just learn one meaning of a new word; expand your vocabulary quickly by learning how to use the **same** word in **different** ways.

These sentences show some of the ways in which the word '**come**' can be used. Complete each sentence by using **come** (or **came**) and one of the words below. Use each of these words once only.

| across | from | out | undone |
|--------|------|-----|--------|
| along | off | over | up |

1. Don't stay indoors all day! . . . . . . . . . . . . . . . . for a walk.
2. I . . . . . . . . . . . . . . . this letter in the drawer of my desk.
3. . . . . . . . . . . . . . . . ., children, or we'll be late!
4. She hurt her shoulder when she . . . . . . . . . . . . . . . . her horse.
5. What's . . *came* . . *over* . . . him? He never used to be like this.
6. I . . . . . . . . . . . . . . . Edinburgh, the capital of Scotland.
7. The water in the river only . . *came up* . . . . . . to our knees.
8. Oh no! My shoelaces have . . *come* . . *undone* . . . again!

Now do the same with the following words to complete sentences. Use part of the verb **get** and one of these words:

| into | on | ready | up |
|------|-----|-------|-----|
| off | over | tired | used |

9. How do you . . . . . . . . . . . . . . . with your neighbours?
10. I'm . . . . . . . . . . . . . . . of all these interruptions!
11. He's still in bed. Why hasn't he . . . . . . . . . . . . . . . yet?
12. I'm busy . . . . . . . . the house . . . . . . . . for the party.
13. It took her two months to . . . . . . . . . . . . . . . the operation.
14. He . . . . . . . . . . . . . . . a lot of trouble for breaking the chair.
15. . . *Got off* . . . . . . . . the bus at the town hall.
16. I still haven't . . . *got* . . *used* . . . . . to this climate.

14

# 9 Crosswords

Here are some very small crosswords. Can you complete them? You might need to check one or two answers in your dictionary.

## Crossword 1

**Across**
1. The . . . . . . . . of the pudding is in the eating. (Proverb)
4. He's perfect. He's the . . . . . . . . man for the job.
5. I don't like this cheese. It's got a very strange . . . . . . . . .

**Down**
1. Please . . . . . . . . in block capitals.
2. Where one door shuts, another . . . . . . . . . (Proverb)
3. Untrue.

## Crossword 2

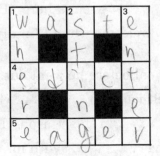

**Across**
1. . . . . . . . . not, want not. (Proverb)
4. If you don't pay your rent, your landlord will . . . . . . . . you.
5. Keen and enthusiastic.

**Down**
1. . . . . . . . . there's a will, there's a way. (Proverb)
2. Everything he said was nice, but of course there was a . . . . . . . . in the tail.
3. Come on, you've got to . . . . . . . . into the spirit of the occasion.

15

# 10 Opposites – 1

When you see an adjective in a sentence, ask yourself if it is possible to replace it by its opposite. Where it is possible, you will notice that some adjectives have several opposites depending on the context.

The opposite of 'old' for example, could be 'new' or 'young' depending on the situation. Can you think of any more examples like this? Asking yourself questions about your own English—what you **do** know, and what you **don't** know—will help you to improve more quickly.

Complete each sentence with the opposite of the word in brackets. Choose from one of the following words. Use each word once only.

| | | | |
|---|---|---|---|
| alcoholic | light | public | smooth |
| cool | permanent | sensible | strong |
| generous | present | shallow | thick |
| high | professional | sharp | tight |

1. The student you mentioned is . . . . . . . . today. (ABSENT)

2. The match was between two . . . . . . . . teams. (AMATEUR)

3. He separated the . . . . . . . . . knives from the others. (BLUNT)

4. The water is quite . . . . . . . . around here. (DEEP)

5. I got a very . . . . . . . . welcome when I finally arrived. (ENTHUSIASTIC)

6. He had a . . . . . . . . meal before he went out. (HEAVY)

7. Are you sure your belt isn't too . . . . . . . . ? (LOOSE)

8. The risk of fire is . . . . . . . . in this season. (LOW)

9. The millionaire was very . . . . . . . . with his tips. (MEAN)

10. They told me this was a . . . . . . . . footpath. (PRIVATE)

11. She's got such . . . . . . . . skin. (ROUGH)

12. They don't serve . . . . . . . . drinks. (SOFT)

13. Some of them asked very . . . . . . . . questions. (STUPID)

14. I'm looking for a . . . . . . . . job. (TEMPORARY)

15. He cut himself a . . . . . . . . slice of bread. (THIN)

16. She always drinks . . . . . . . . tea. (WEAK)

16

# 11 In the office

Look at the picture of an office. On the list below, number each item which is numbered in the picture.

| ....... briefcase | ....... desk | ....... rubber |
| ....... calculator | ....... files | ....... ruler |
| ....... calendar | ....... filing cabinet | ....... scissors |
| ....... chair | ....... pad | ....... telephone |
| ....... clock | ....... pencil | ....... tray |
| ....... computer | ....... plant | ....... waste paper bin |

# 12 Confusing words – 1

If you use a word in the wrong way, learn from your mistake. Find out what the correct word or expression should be and then use both the correct and incorrect words in sentences so that you can understand and remember the difference.

Choose the correct word for each sentence.

1. The others can't come so you'll have to go **alone/lonely.**
2. She's sitting over there **among/between** those two boys.
3. He was very **asleep/sleepy** so he went to bed early.
4. Can I **borrow/lend** £10? I'll pay you back tomorrow.
5. They were **delighted/delightful** that she had won.
6. She's been away **for/since** two days now.
7. I was very **interested/interesting** in what he said.
8. I'm looking for a **job/work** with a higher salary.
9. They went on a long **journey/travel** around Africa.
10. The students had some English **homework/housework** to do.
11. He **laid/lay** down on the sand and went to sleep.
12. Don't wear green. It doesn't **match/suit** you.
13. He put up a big **note/notice** advertising the concert.
14. It's **quiet/quite** difficult to understand what he says.
15. This weather **remembers/reminds** me of home.
16. They **robbed/stole** him of all his money.
17. The bus leaves from the **station/stop** nearest the office.
18. That's the man **whose/who's** dog bit me.

When you are sure you know the correct word, cross out the wrong one. Make your own sentences using the words so that you can learn how to use them properly.

# 13 Word wheel

Fill the wheel, using the clues. Each five-letter word starts at the edge of the wheel and ends in the centre.
As you can see, they all end in the same letter.

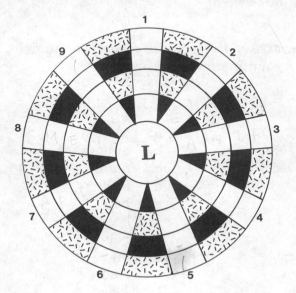

1. The opposite of urban.
2. A place to stay when you're away from home.
3. It means the same as *last*.
4. What an . . . . . . . . day! You'll need your umbrella.
5. Confined to a small area; near home.    *local*
6. Of the same size or volume.
7. Mind you don't . . . . . . . . your tea. The cup is very full.
8. What's that dreadful . . . . . . . . ? Is something burning on the stove?
9. What size do you think this is? It doesn't say on the . . . . . . . . . .

It always helps to learn vocabulary in groups — around a theme; beginning with the same letter; objects in the same picture etc. Lists are not easy to remember. Try to arrange the words you want to learn in a shape or around a theme. It really helps!

# 14 Word partnerships – 2

Remember to look out for pairs of words which often occur together. If you
meet one, you can expect the other. This makes it easier to understand
written and spoken English.

Match each adjective on the left with a noun on the right. Use each word
once only. Write your answers in the boxes.

## Set 1

| | | | | | |
|---|---|---|---|---|---|
| 1. | bald | a. | accent | 1 | |
| 2. | complete | b. | atmosphere | 2 | |
| 3. | crowded | c. | failure | 3 | |
| 4. | deep | d. | food | 4 | |
| 5. | fatal | e. | hair | 5 | |
| 6. | relaxed | f. | head | 6 | |
| 7. | spicy | g. | hole | 7 | |
| 8. | strong | h. | injury | 8 | |
| 9. | wavy | i. | train | 9 | |
| 10. | woollen | j. | sweater | 10 | |

## Set 2
Now do the same with these words

| | | | | | |
|---|---|---|---|---|---|
| 1. | anonymous | a. | advantage | 1 | |
| 2. | balanced | b. | bread | 2 | |
| 3. | busy | c. | breeze | 3 | |
| 4. | electric | d. | cooker | 4 | |
| 5. | enthusiastic | e. | dictionary | 5 | |
| 6. | flat | f. | diet | 6 | |
| 7. | gentle | g. | tyre | 7 | |
| 8. | monolingual | h. | letter | 8 | |
| 9. | sliced | i. | office | 9 | |
| 10. | unfair | j. | welcome | 10 | |

20

# 15 What's missing?

Under each picture write the name of the item and what is missing.
Choose from the following list of words.
The first has been done for you.

| | | |
|---|---|---|
| baby buggy | crane | strings |
| back | ears | switches |
| bike | kangaroo | television |
| broom | handle | violin |
| butterfly | handlebars | wheel |
| chair | hook | wing |

1..... *chair* ..........
...... *back* ..........

2..... broom ..........
..... handle ......

3..... butterfly .....
........ wing ........

4.................
....... ears .......

5.................
...... wheel ......

6..... television .....
...... switches ......

7..... violin ..........
...... strings ..........

8..... crane ..........
...... hook ..........

9..... bike ..........
..... handlebars ......

21

# 16 Phrasal verbs – 1

By matching the numbers with the letters find the phrasal verbs with the meanings given.

| 1 BREAK | | 2 CARRY | | 3 JOIN |
|---|---|---|---|---|
| | 4 FIND | | 5 TURN | |
| 6 CALL | | 7 GET | | 8 COME |
| | 9 PASS | | 10 GO | |
| A OFF | | B IN | | C ON |
| | D OVER | | E AWAY | |
| F ACROSS | | G WITH | | H INTO |
| | I OUT | | J UP | |

| | | |
|---|---|---|
| ARRIVE | 5 | |
| CANCEL | | A |
| CONTINUE | 2 | |
| DIE | | E |
| DISCOVER | 4 | |
| ENTER BY FORCE | | H |
| FIND BY CHANCE | 8 | |
| MATCH | | G |
| PARTICIPATE | 3 | |
| RECOVER | | D |

Use the phrasal verbs to complete each of these sentences:

**1.** Does this jacket . . . . . . . . . . . . . . . . my trousers?

**2.** I wish I could . . . . . . . . . . . . . . . . the truth.

**3.** If you . . . . . . . . . . . . . . . . . . . . . . . . . . . . . . . . . . up . . . . . late for work, you're going to get into trouble. (2 phrasal verbs here)

**4.** We had to . . . . . . . . . . . . . . . . our holiday because my wife was taken into hospital the day before our intended departure.

**5.** While I was tidying up, I . . . . . . . . . . . . . . . . these old photos.

**6.** The burglar . . . . . . . . . . . . . . . . the house while the owner was away on holiday.

**7.** Is this a private matter or can anyone . . . . . . . . . . . . . . . . ?

**8.** She's lived alone since her husband . . . . . . . . . . . . . . . . .

**9.** It's taken her a long time to . . . . . . . . . . . . . . . . the tragedy.

# 17 Menu

Arranging words in lists in easy, but lists are very difficult to remember. One way of organising words so that they are more memorable is to draw a diagram like the one below.

Why don't you try and do a similar diagram for other words which can be grouped together in this way? You could try this with subjects like *the house, sport or education*.

In this exercise you have to complete the diagram by using words from the following list. Use each word once only.

| | | | |
|---|---|---|---|
| alcoholic | fish | peach | tea |
| carrots | lamb chop | red | trout |
| chips | meat | roast beef | vanilla |
| desserts | medium | soup | white |

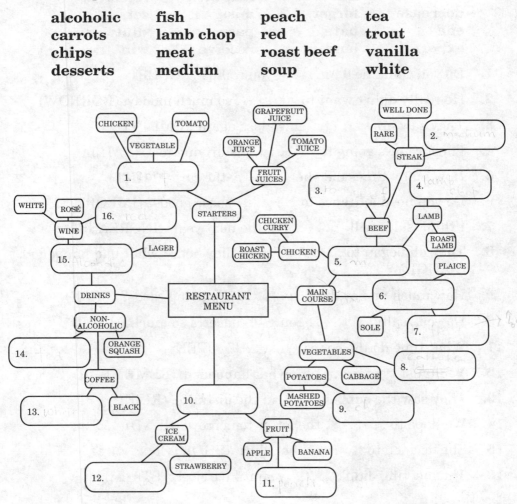

# 18 Opposites – 2

You can often build your vocabulary by asking yourself if you know the **opposite** of one of the most important words in a sentence.

It also helps to learn words in a complete sentence. This makes them easier to remember.

Complete each sentence with the opposite of the word in brackets. Choose from one of the following words. Use each word once only.

| | | | |
|---|---|---|---|
| cry | fill | lengthen | reject |
| decrease | forget | miss | set |
| end | hate | pass | shut |
| export | lend | receive | win |

1.  Do you think he'll . . . . . . . . your offer? (ACCEPT)

2.  He really didn't want to . . . . . . . . so much money. (BORROW)

3.  They saw him . . . . . . . . his glass again. (EMPTY)

4.  I'm sure he's going to . . . . . . . . his driving test. (FAIL)

5.  How many times did she . . . . . . . . the target? (HIT)

6.  Do you need a licence to . . . . . . . . these goods? (IMPORT)

7.  I think sales will . . . . . . . . in the next year. (INCREASE)

8.  They all began to . . . . . . . . when they heard what had happened. (LAUGH)

9.  How much money did you . . . . . . . . playing cards? (LOSE)

10. Do you really . . . . . . . . going to concerts so much? (LOVE)

11. What time do the shops . . . . . . . . ? (OPEN)

12. You must try to . . . . . . . . what happened. (REMEMBER)

13. They saw the sun . . . . . . . . in the distance. (RISE)

14. We hope to . . . . . . . . the letter tomorrow. (SEND)

15. She decided to . . . . . . . . her skirt. (SHORTEN)

16. The meeting didn't . . . . . . . . until 6 o'clock. (START)

# 19 Visiting

Put each of the following conversations in the right order. Each contains useful language if you are visiting someone in their home.

1.   **a.** Not at all. Come on in.
       **b.** I've brought you a few flowers.
       **c.** Hi. I hope I'm not too early.
       **d.** Oh, how nice! You didn't need to do that.

2.   **a.** Thanks.
       **b.** Have you got a beer?
       **c.** Now, what can I get you to drink?
       **d.** Let me put your coat somewhere.

3.   **a.** Yes, I suppose we have really.
       **b.** Thanks. We like it.
       **c.** And you've got a great view, haven't you?
       **d.** I like the way you've done the house.

4.   **a.** This is very nice.
       **b.** Well, perhaps just a little.
       **c.** I'm glad you like it. Have some more if you like.
       **d.** And help yourself to salad.

5.   **a.** No, not for me, thanks.
       **b.** Oh, go on then.
       **c.** Another glass of wine?
       **d.** Are you sure?

6.   **a.** Is that the time? I'd no idea it was so late. I must be going soon.
       **b.** No, I'm all right, thanks.
       **c.** Would you like another coffee before you go?
       **d.** Right. I'll just go and get your coat then.

7.   **a.** You must come over to our place next time.
       **b.** Thank you for a lovely evening.
       **c.** Yes, that'd be nice. Bye then. Drive carefully.
       **d.** I'm glad you enjoyed it.

The above expressions are exactly the things you will hear native speakers of English say. If you use them yourself, it is important to get them absolutely right – otherwise, you may change their meaning entirely.

# 20 Several meanings

When you look up a word in a dictionary, don't just look at the first definition. See if the word has more than one meaning. Sometimes the meanings will be connected, sometimes not. You can build your vocabulary by learning extra meanings for words you already know.

In this exercise you will see pairs of sentences with the same word missing. You have to decide what the word is. Choose from the following list.

| bank | course | ring | star |
|------|--------|------|------|
| block | head | service | tank |
| cabin | note | shade | tap |
| change | present | spot | trunk |

1  a.  I'm sleeping in the best . . . . . . . . . in the ship.

   b.  He lived in a little . . . . . . . . in the forest.

2  a.  We both had steak for the main . . . . . . . . . .

   b.  My English . . . . . . . . lasts for three months.

3  a.  The hat wouldn't fit on his . . . . . . . . . .

   b.  The . . . . . . . . of the company is visiting us tomorrow.

4  a.  The singer had difficulty reaching the top . . . . . . . . . .

   b.  She left him a . . . . . . . . saying she'd be late.

5  a.  I work in the large office . . . . . . . . near the station.

   b.  He used a . . . . . . . . of wood to keep the door open.

6  a.  We always get good . . . . . . . . in this shop.

   b.  She's gone to the evening . . . . . . . . at the church.

7  a.  There was a . . . . . . . . in the middle of his forehead.

   b.  This looks like a good . . . . . . . for a picnic.

8  a.  They sat in the . . . . . . . . of a tall tree.

   b.  I don't really like that . . . . . . . . of blue.

**9** **a.** There were three men fishing from the river . . . . . . . . .

**b.** I asked my . . . . . . . manager to lend me £2,000.

**10** **a.** Suddenly there was a . . . . . . . at the front door.

**b.** I lost my wedding . . . . . . . in the back garden.

**11** **a.** The elephant waved its . . . . . . . at the visitors.

**b.** He sat on a fallen tree . . . . . . . to watch the birds.

**12** **a.** That's all the news we have at . . . . . . . . .

**b.** What are you getting her as a birthday . . . . . . . ?

**13** **a.** Our new . . . . . . . has a more powerful gun.

**b.** Fill up your . . . . . . . before your journey.

**14** **a.** The . . . . . . . shone high in the sky.

**b.** A famous film . . . . . . . opened the exhibition.

**15** **a.** I heard a soft . . . . . . . on the kitchen door.

**b.** There isn't any water coming from this . . . . . . . !

**16** **a.** I need some . . . . . . . for the drinks machine.

**b.** This year we're going to the seaside for a . . . . . . . . .

**There was a soft tap on the kitchen door.**

# 21 Product information–1

If you can get newspapers or magazines in English, look at the advertisements. You can find a lot of useful vocabulary in them.

In addition, many products have information written in English which will also help you to build your vocabulary. Remember, there are many opportunities to see real English. All of them can help you to learn.

In this exercise you will see some information about a product. You must decide which product is being referred to. Choose the product from the following list. Each product is referred to once only.

| | | | |
|---|---|---|---|
| **briefcase** | **film** | **kitchen scales** | **television** |
| **clock** | **frying pan** | **pen** | **tent** |
| **cosmetic set** | **hair drier** | **rug** | **tyre pump** |
| **electric heater** | **handbag** | **sunglasses** | **video recorder** |

Lined interior, document folio in lid. Combination locks. Size 17x12x4 inch approx.

1. . . . . . . . . . . . . . . . . .

Black numerals and hands. Metal case. Height 4 inch approx.

2. . . . . . . . . . . . . . . . . .

All steel construction. With dial pressure gauge reading 0-60 psi. Universal fitting.

3. . . . . . . . . . . . . . . . . .

Contains 10 powder eyeshadows, 3 powder blushers, 1 highlighter, 4 lip gloss, 1 waterproof mascara,

4. . . . . . . . . . . . . . . . . .

Pre-programming of up to 4 events over 14 days. HQ feature for enhanced picture quality, electronic tracking controls and quick record facility.

5. . . . . . . . . . . . . . . . . .

Weighs up to 6lb 10oz/3kg by 1oz/20g graduations. Zero adjusting facility for weighing each ingredient.

6. . . . . . . . . . . . . . . . . .

Fully lined with interior compartment
and pocket. Detachable strap.

12 inch (V30cm) model. Rotary controls for
tuning,on/off/volume, brightness and contrast.

7. . . . . . . . . . . . . . . . . .

8. . . . . . . . . . . . . . . . . .

1600 watt. Lightweight. 4 heat/speed
combinations. Clip-on styling nozzle.

For gas or radiant ring.

9. . . . . . . . . . . . . . . . . .

10. . . . . . . . . . . . . . . . . .

Made from specially toughened glass. The
lenses also protect eyes from ultra violet
radiation..

Processing included in price. For colour slides.
36 exposures.

11. . . . . . . . . . . . . . . . . .

12. . . . . . . . . . . . . . . . . .

For picnics, car or home. Fully washable. 80%
acrylic/20% other fibres. Size 51x67 inch.

Ideal for up to five people.

13. . . . . . . . . . . . . . . . . .

14. . . . . . . . . . . . . . . . . .

Blue with stainless steel trim.
Blue ink.

Variable thermostat control. Freestanding or
wall mounted.

15. . . . . . . . . . . . . . . . . .

16. . . . . . . . . . . . . . . . . .

# 22 The weather

In this exercise notice the words which help you to guess the answer. One word in a sentence or article often helps you guess others. Good guessing helps you to learn!

Complete each sentence by choosing the best alternative.
Look up any words you are not sure about.

1. They saw . . . . . . . . of snow falling slowly to the ground.
   **a.** blocks **b.** piles **c.** flakes **d.** floods

2. We drove very slowly because the . . . . . . . . was so thick.
   **a.** sunshine **b.** lightning **c.** fog **d.** avalanche

3. The heavy rain caused . . . . . . . . all over the country.
   **a.** drought **b.** flooding **c.** tides **d.** fountains

4. The tree fell to the ground after lightning . . . . . . . . it.
   **a.** soaked **b.** beat **c.** struck **d.** burst

5. Those . . . . . . . . in the sky mean it's going to rain.
   **a.** frosts **b.** flakes **c.** mists **d.** clouds

6. That . . . . . . . . should dry my washing.
   **a.** gust **b.** puff **c.** blizzard **d.** breeze

7. The top of the mountain was . . . . . . . . in mist.
   **a.** covered **b.** condensed **c.** vaporised **d.** drenched

8. The hurricane . . . . . . . . several buildings on the island.
   **a.** exhausted **b.** destroyed **c.** blew up **d.** condensed

9. They could hear the thunder . . . . . . . . in the distance.
   **a.** grumbling **b.** drifting **c.** pouring **d.** rumbling

10. Look how white the grass is! Is that snow or . . . . . . . . ?
    **a.** dew **b.** mist **c.** steam **d.** frost

11. When the sun came out, the ice slowly . . . . . . . . . . .
    **a.** melted **b.** flooded **c.** froze **d.** dried

12. It's . . . . . . . . outside, so take your overcoat.
    **a.** mild **b.** sweltering **c.** stuffy **d.** chilly

13. The gale . . . . . . . . all night.
    **a.** poured **b.** died down **c.** blew **d.** puffed

14. Be quiet! This is the weather . . . . . . . . for the weekend.
    **a.** forecast **b.** broadcast **c.** prophecy **d.** horoscope

15. It's only . . . . . . . . so I won't take my umbrella.
    **a.** pouring **b.** hailing **c.** sleeting **d.** drizzling

# 23 Rhymes

Knowing how to pronounce a word is sometimes a problem. It may be difficult at first, but it is a good idea to learn the symbols used for the different sounds in English. A good dictionary should have a list of the symbols it uses. You can then look up the pronunciation of any word you are not sure about. Remember you don't really know a word until you know how to pronounce it.

Which of the words on the right does **not** rhyme with the word on the left?

| | | | | | |
|---|---|---|---|---|---|
| 1. | alone | phone | shown | thrown | town |
| 2. | buys | advise | price | prize | tries |
| 3. | clear | bear | beer | dear | fear |
| 4. | could | good | mood | should | wood |
| 5. | goes | chose | lose | shows | toes |
| 6. | knees | niece | peas | please | trees |
| 7. | knew | grew | sew | threw | through |
| 8. | made | afraid | paid | played | said |
| 9. | most | cost | post | roast | toast |
| 10. | route | boot | foot | shoot | suit |
| 11. | shoes | choose | does | lose | news |
| 12. | son | fun | on | sun | won |
| 13. | there | care | hair | here | wear |
| 14. | thumb | come | home | some | sum |
| 15. | throw | go | know | toe | too |
| 16. | weight | great | height | late | straight |
| 17. | word | bird | heard | lord | third |
| 18. | worse | horse | nurse | purse | reverse |

# 24 'Make' or 'do'?

There are a number of expressions in English with 'make' or 'do'.
You often 'make' **something** but use 'do' to describe an **action**; sometimes
it isn't so easy to know which one to use.
If you look up one of these expressions in a dictionary you will sometimes
find the expression under 'make' or 'do'. Sometimes , however, you have to
look under the other part of the expression. For question 6 in this exercise,
for example, you should find the expression if you look under the word
'decision'.

Complete each sentence with the correct form of 'make' or 'do'. Make
sure you use the correct tense!

1. What do you . . . . . . . . for a living? — I'm a dentist.

2. He . . . . . . . . a big mistake when he changed his job.

3. You look very tired. Would you like me . . . . . . . . you a cup of
   coffee?

4. What have I . . . . . . . . with my handbag? I can't find it anywhere!

5. I haven't got a £20 note. Will two £10 notes . . . . . . . . ?

6. Why does it take them so long . . . . . . . . decisions?

7. They . . . . . . . . fun of him whenever he wore his new hat.

8. That will . . . . . . . . , children! You're giving me a terrible
   headache!

9. Why does she . . . . . . . . such a fuss of him?

10. What have you . . . . . . . . to this table cloth? It's got some kind of
    red liquid all over it!

11. Don't forget to . . . . . . . . your hair before you go out.

12. Could you . . . . . . . . me a favour? Please drive me to town.

13. This car is very economical. It . . . . . . . . 40 miles to the gallon.

14. He had difficulty . . . . . . . . his way through the crowd.

15. It's very important to . . . . . . . . a good impression at this meeting.

16. Please . . . . . . . . sure you've switched off all the lights before you leave.

17. This room could . . . . . . . with a good clean.

18. Please sit down and . . . . . . . . yourself at home.

19. Don't have anything to . . . . . . . . with him. He can't be trusted.

20. When he was younger, he . . . . . . . . a fortune selling clothes.

21. I think the answer is 2,376. What do you . . . . . . . it?

22. How would you like your steak . . . . . . . . ? — Medium, please.

23. He . . . . . . . . so much noise that he woke her up.

24. She wasn't very happy about . . . . . . . . without sugar in her coffee.

25. The new manager . . . . . . . . some changes as soon as he arrived.

26. It doesn't matter if you don't come first as long as you . . . . . . . . your best.

27. I want to . . . . . . . . a phone call. Have you got any change?

28. How did you . . . . . . . . in your exam? — Quite well, I think.

29. Have a nice cup of tea. It will . . . . . . . . you good.

30. Take this medicine. It will . . . . . . . . you better.

31. What time do you . . . . . . . . it? — Nearly six o'clock.

32. Be quiet! Don't . . . . . . . . a sound!

> Remember many expressions containing **make** or **do** are word partnerships — you need to learn the whole expression.
>
> Go through the examples above and underline the special expressions you can find.

When you are sure you know the correct answers, make two lists, one for 'make' and one for 'do' and do your best to make your own examples using the expressions you have listed.

# 25 Two-word expressions

Sometimes in English two words are used together to make a common expression, for example:

credit card               vacuum cleaner

Sometimes you find these expressions listed separately in a dictionary and sometimes they are included in the definitions of one, or both, of the two words.

Join one word on the left with one from the right to make a two-word partnership. Use each word once only. Write your answers in the boxes.

| | | | | | |
|---|---|---|---|---|---|
| 1. | car | a. | aid | 1 | |
| 2. | civil | b. | band | 2 | |
| 3. | common | c. | board | 3 | |
| 4. | department | d. | box | 4 | |
| 5. | first | e. | card | 5 | |
| 6. | notice | f. | clip | 6 | |
| 7. | paper | g. | lights | 7 | |
| 8. | playing | h. | machine | 8 | |
| 9. | pocket | i. | money | 9 | |
| 10. | post | j. | office | 10 | |
| 11. | rubber | k. | park | 11 | |
| 12. | safety | l. | pin | 12 | |
| 13. | telephone | m. | sense | 13 | |
| 14. | trade | n. | service | 14 | |
| 15. | traffic | o. | store | 15 | |
| 16. | washing | p. | union | 16 | |

Did you find any other possible combinations while you were doing the exercise? Can you think of any more words to go with those on the left?

Remember, learning word partnerships — words which go together — is just as important as learning new words.

# 26 Situations

Put each of the following dialogues in the right order.

1. **Congratulations**
   **a.** Oh, yes. I <u>got</u> the results yesterday.
   **b.** Thanks very much.
   **c.** Congratulations! Well done.
   **d.** Oh, by the way, I hear you did very well (in) your exams.

2. **Mistaken Identity**
   **a.** That's all right.
   **b.** I'm sorry, I don't think we've met.
   **c.** Hello. It's David Wright, isn't it? Remember me?
   **d.** Oh, I'm terribly sorry. I thought you were <u>someone else.</u>

3. **Starting a Conversation**
   **a.** That's right. I lived in Aranjuez, actually. Do you know Spain at all?
   **b.** Oh, really. That's a coincidence. I might know her. What did you say your name was?
   **c.** I heard you spent some time in Spain. Madrid, wasn't it?
   **d.** Well, I know Aranjuez. In fact, my sister lives there, funnily enough.

4. **Finishing a Conversation**
   **a.** Nice talking to you too. Can I get you another drink?
   **b.** Of course. It's been nice talking to you.
   **c.** No, I'm all right at the moment, thanks.
   **d.** If you'll excuse me, I must just go and say hello to some people I know.

5. **Weekends**
   **a.** Well, we thought we'd go to London – see a show or something. . .
   **b.** No, not really. How about you?
   **c.** So, have you got any plans for the weekend?
   **d.** Oh, that'll be nice. Perhaps we should do something like that instead of the same old thing.

6. **Goodbyes**
   **a.** Right, I think that's everything packed. Thanks very much for everything.
   **b.** Bye. Don't forget to write!
   **c.** Oh, that sounds like our taxi. Thanks again. Bye, then.
   **d.** Not at all. It's been a pleasure.

# 27 Entertainment

Remember that making lists related to topics will help you to learn vocabulary. This exercise on entertainment should give you some ideas. As you think of more vocabulary related to the topic you could make separate lists under headings such as music, the theatre, the cinema, television etc.

Find the correct words for the people in the pictures and also to complete the sentences. Choose from the following list. Use each word once only.

| | | | |
|---|---|---|---|
| announcer | critic | LP | scriptwriter |
| audience | disc jockey | magician | spotlight |
| balcony | drummer | opera | string |
| ballet dancer | guitarist | orchestra | studio |
| cinema | interval | rehearsal | tune |
| clown | joke | row | understudy |
| conductor | juggler | scene | ventriloquist |

1. . . . . . . . . . . . . . . . .

2. . . . . . . . . . . . . . . . .

3. . . . . . . . . . . . . . . . .

4. . . . . . . . . . . . . .

5. . . . . . . . . . . . . . .

6. . . . . . . . . . . . . . . .

7. . . . . . . . . . . . . . .

8. . . . . . . . . . . . . . .

9. . . . . . . . . . . . . . .

Notice how in the sentences below you can guess the word you are looking for from other related words, for example, 'applauded' in the first sentence. Underline words like this and add them to your lists of vocabulary.

10. The . . . . . . . . all applauded when she came onto the stage.

11. What film is on at the . . . . . . . . this week?

12. I watched a concert given by a famous symphony . . . . . . . . . .

13. I always get a seat in the . . . . . . . . when I go to the theatre. I can see much better from up there.

14. There was just one . . . . . . . . on the singer. The rest of the stage was in darkness.

15. I didn't think the . . . . . . . . he told was at all funny.

16. The . . . . . . . . apologised to viewers for the delay.

17. The dress- . . . . . . . . was terrible. Let's hope the first night will be much better.

18. The . . . . . . . . in the newspaper said it was the best film of the year.

19. After ten hours in the recording . . . . . . . . , the group were finally satisfied.

20. The director asked the . . . . . . . . to change some of the lines in the first part of the film.

21. When the leading man became ill, his . . . . . . . . . . had to take his place.

22. As soon as the lights went up for the . . . . . . . . , the children rushed to the front to buy ice creams.

23. Not all . . . . . . . . singers are large, you know!

24. I've got us two seats in . . . . . . . . D, near the front.

25. In the final . . . . . . . . of the film, the hero rode off into the sunset.

26. A . . . . . . . . broke as she was playing her violin.

27. That piano sounds out of . . . . . . . . to me!

28. Her latest . . . . . . . . contains a new extended version of her hit record.

# 28 Health – 1

Choose the best alternative to complete the sentence.
Look up any words you don't know.

1. He's over 90 but he's very . . . . . . . . . . for his age.
   **a.** tense     **b.** nervous     **c.** active     **d.** uneasy

2. The nurse wrapped a . . . . . . . . . . round my head.
   **a.** bandage     **b.** plaster     **c.** cream     **d.** pain-killer

3. They run every day to keep . . . . . . . . .
   **a.** fat     **b.** fit     **c.** faint     **d.** upset

4. Her leg was very painful after the insect . . . . . . . . . . it.
   **a.** inflamed     **b.** stung     **c.** stabbed     **d.** blistered

5. Can you recommend some medicine for a dry . . . . . . . . . .?
   **a.** cold     **b.** headache     **c.** sneeze     **d.** cough

6. She . . . . . . . . . . a muscle while lifting some furniture.
   **a.** broke     **b.** fractured     **c.** pulled     **d.** cut

7. I'm sure his illness was caused by . . . . . . . . .
   **a.** overwork     **b.** stamina     **c.** fitness     **d.** health

8. If my toothache continues, I'll see my . . . . . . . . . .
   **a.** optician     **b.** vet     **c.** dentist     **d.** surgeon

9. You can only get this medicine on . . . . . . . . . .
   **a.** description     **b.** hospital     **c.** prescription     **d.** allergy

10. He went on a diet because of his high blood . . . . . . . . . .
    **a.** tension     **b.** pressure     **c.** poisoning     **d.** inflammation

11. His wife gave him . . . . . . . . , which saved his life.
    **a.** sunburn     **b.** a tonic     **c.** dandruff     **d.** first aid

12. Where's the . . . . . . . . . .? I want to take my temperature.
    **a.** meter     **b.** stethoscope     **c.** antiseptic     **d.** thermometer

13. The surgeon operated . . . . . . . . . . his leg yesterday.
    **a.** on     **b.** with     **c.** for     **d.** in

14. I must buy some pastilles for my sore . . . . . . . . . .
    **a.** knee     **b.** thumb     **c.** throat     **d.** ankle

15. I'm a bit . . . . . . . . so could you speak a little louder?
    **a.** dumb     **b.** blind     **c.** deaf     **d.** lame

16. We're going to . . . . . . . . . . you with a different kind of drug, which we hope will be more successful.
    **a.** cure     **b.** treat     **c.** intoxicate     **d.** heal

# 29 Classified ads

Below you will see the first parts of some advertisements. Decide which classification each one should appear under.
Use each classification only once.

**ACCOMMODATION**   **EDUCATION**   **MEDICAL**
**BABY & NURSERY**   **FURNITURE**   **MUSICAL**
**BOATS**   **GARDENING**   **PERSONAL**
**CLAIRVOYANTS**   **HOLIDAYS & TRAVEL**   **PHOTOGRAPHY**

ENGLISH tuition, foreign students, experienced teacher.

**1.** . . . . . . . . . . . . . . . .

ROCKING CHAIR as new. £40.

**2.** . . . . . . . . . . . . . . .

A SECOND PERSON wanted to share modern terraced house.

**3.** . . . . . . . . . . . . . . .

QUALIFIED CHIROPODIST, surgery or home visits.

**4.** . . . . . . . . . . . . . . .

BUDGET airfares. European and world wide.

**5.** . . . . . . . . . . . . . . .

ANITA palmist and medium. Consultations day/evening.

**6.** . . . . . . . . . . . . . . .

ANCHOR — 25lbs. Unused.

**7.** . . . . . . . . . . . . . . .

FOR SALE cot and mattress, good condition.

**8.** . . . . . . . . . . . . . . .

SHRUBS and conifers from £1 each.

**9.** . . . . . . . . . . . . . . .

TEACHER, young 50, seeks companion for evenings out.

**10.** . . . . . . . . . . . . . . .

A BEST PRICE for all pianos, any condition.

**11.** . . . . . . . . . . . . . . .

CASH paid for cameras, lenses, accessories.

**12.** . . . . . . . . . . . . . . .

# 30 Money – 1

Choose the best word to complete the sentence.
Look up any words you do not know.

1.  Last January the train . . . . . . . . went up by 7%.
    **a.** taxes      **b.** fares      **c.** fees      **d.** premiums

2.  He was . . . . . . . . $400 for driving dangerously.
    **a.** found      **b.** retired      **c.** loaned      **d.** fined

3.  If you buy twenty or more, you'll get a . . . . . . . . .
    **a.** discount      **b.** loss      **c.** reject      **d.** budget

4.  She was very pleased because she made a . . . . . . . . of £10,000 on the sale of her house.
    **a.** loss      **b.** profit      **c.** fortune      **d.** benefit

5.  Take the . . . . . . . . if you want them to change the shirt.
    **a.** recipe      **b.** register      **c.** receipt      **d.** repayment

6.  He spent all the money he had won . . . . . . . . new clothes.
    **a.** on      **b.** for      **c.** with      **d.** from

7.  I need some . . . . . . . . for the coffee machine.
    **a.** exchange      **b.** bills      **c.** change      **d.** finance

8.  The mechanic didn't . . . . . . . . me for repairing my car.
    **a.** change      **b.** charge      **c.** bribe      **d.** tax

9.  She let the family live in the cottage . . . . . . . . free.
    **a.** hire      **b.** accommodation      **c.** let      **d.** rent

10. The contents of the shop were insured . . . . . . . . £500,000.
    **a.** for      **b.** until      **c.** on      **d.** from

11. I'm going to ask my bank manager for a . . . . . . . . . .
    **a.** lend      **b.** borrow      **c.** loan      **d.** finance

12. Is it all right if I pay . . . . . . . . cheque?
    **a.** by      **b.** in      **c.** on      **d.** from

13. The mark has risen in . . . . . . . . against the dollar.
    **a.** exchange      **b.** value      **c.** currency      **d.** change

14. So many people buy things . . . . . . . . credit nowadays.
    **a.** on      **b.** by      **c.** in      **d.** from

15. The more I earn, the more . . . . . . . . tax I pay.
    **a.** salary      **b.** wages      **c.** income      **d.** expenditure

16. If you aren't satisfied, we'll . . . . . . . . your money.
    **a.** put away      **b.** put aside      **c.** refund      **d.** reduce

# 31 Name the part

Under each picture write the name of the creature and the part the
arrow points to. Choose from the following lists of words. Use each word
once only. /raiˈnɒsərəs/

| | | | |
|---|---|---|---|
| **rhinoceros** | **elephant** | **horn** 马嘴 | **trunk** |
| **horse** | **squirrel** | **hoof** | **tail** |
| **parrot** | **tortoise** | **beak** [biːk] | **shell** |
| **crab** | **bear** [bɔːə] | **claw** | **paw** |
| **ostrich** ostri | | **feathers** | |

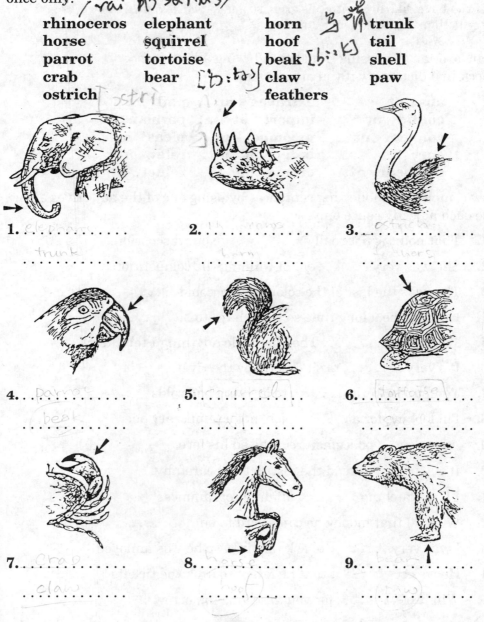

1. elephant

trunk

2. rhinoceros

horn

3. ostrich

feathers

4. parrot

beak

5. squirrel

6. tortoise

7. crab

claw

8. horse

hoof

9. bear

claw

# 32 Important adjectives

Spelling is often a problem in English. It is a good idea to make a list of words that you find difficult to spell and test yourself regularly on them.

If you have difficulty with this exercise, make two lists with the words and try to think of some more examples.

Is an 'a' or an 'e' missing from the following adjectives?
Check in a dictionary if you are not sure.

| | | |
|---|---|---|
| abs e nt | extravag a nt | pati e nt |
| confid e nt ✓ | import a nt | permane e nt |
| conveni e nt | incompet a nt | pleas a nt |
| curr e nt | independ e nt | relev a nt |
| disobedi e nt | observ a nt | relucta a nt |

Now complete the following sentences by using one of the adjectives above. Use each adjective once only.

1. That point is not really . . . . . . . . . to our discussion.

2. She was very . . . . . . . . . of winning the competition.

3. This was the last of the colonies to become . . . . . . . . . .

4. He could be a long time so you'll have to be . . . . . . . . . .

5. They're so . . . . . . . . ! They never do anything I tell them!

6. It's very . . . . . . . . to sit quietly by the river.

7. Ten pupils were . . . . . . . . today with bad colds.

8. I'm looking for a . . . . . . . . job, not a temporary one.

9. An . . . . . . . . policeman recognised his face.

10. It's . . . . . . . . to read the instructions carefully.

11. I like watching . . . . . . . . affairs programmes.

12. With all that money he can afford to be . . . . . . . . .

13. I was very . . . . . . . . to ask him in case he was annoyed.

14. He was so . . . . . . . . that he forgot to book the tickets.

15. Will it be . . . . . . . . for you to see me tomorrow?

# 33 Chance meetings

Put each of the following dialogues in the right order:

1. **a.** No, it must be six months or more.
   **b.** Hello Jim. Fancy bumping into you!
   **c.** Oh, at least.
   **d.** Oh, hello. I haven't seen you for ages!

2. **a.** Mm. Still working at the same place, I suppose?
   **b.** Oh, nothing much. The usual things, you know.
   **c.** Yes, that's right.
   **d.** So, what have you been up to?

3. **a.** How about you? What have you and Louise been doing?
   **b.** Yes, the Algarve. We had a great time.
   **c.** Oh really? Did you go somewhere nice?
   **d.** Well, we've just got back from holiday, actually.

4. **a.** Oh, she's fine.
   **b.** Yes, that's right. Oh, they're doing very well.
   **c.** How's Susan then?
   **d.** And the children? Annie and Paul, isn't it?

5. **a.** Yes, it certainly is.
   **b.** Yes, I know. That's why we went away this year.
   **c.** Isn't this weather fantastic?
   **d.** About time too – after all that rain we had.

6. **a.** Oh, that'd be nice. I'll check with her and ring you later.
   **b.** You know, we must get together sometime.
   **c.** Yes, give us a ring and let us know.
   **d.** Yes. I tell you what, why don't you and Susan come over for lunch next Sunday?

> Many of the expressions in these conversations are exactly what native speakers say. If you use them yourself, it is important to get them absolutely right – otherwise, you may change their meaning entirely.

# 34 A recipe

If you have a hobby or interest, use it to help you learn English. See if you know how to talk about it in English. Try to build conversations about it. If there are words you need which you don't know in English, look them up. It is always easier, and more useful to learn what you really **need**.

One interest that many people have is cooking. Can you describe how to make some of your favourite dishes? If not, find out the words you need. This recipe tells you how to make a pancake. You might not make one in exactly the same way. If you don't, see if you can rewrite the instructions.

Fill each of the blanks with the following words. Use each word once.

| | | | |
|---|---|---|---|
| bowl | melt | rest | stir |
| batter | ingredients | serve | turn |
| beat | keep | sift | |
| break | pour | stick | |

**1.** . . . . . . . . for 8 pancakes

| | |
|---|---|
| 125 g flour | About 1 cup milk |
| half teaspoon salt | Fat for frying |
| 1 egg | |

## Method

To avoid getting lumps, **2.** . . . . . . . . the flour and salt into a **3.** . . . . . . . . and make a well in the middle. **4.** . . . . . . . . half the milk into the well and **5.** . . . . . . . . the egg into it. **6.** . . . . . . . . from the middle, gradually mixing in the flour from the sides. Add the **7.** . . . . . . . . of the milk and **8.** . . . . . . . . thoroughly so that everything is well mixed.
**9.** . . . . . . . . a little fat in the bottom of a frying pan. Move it around so that the bottom is evenly covered. When the pan is hot, pour in a little of the **10.** . . . . . . . . . Cook for a minute or two, shaking the pan so that the pancake doesn't **11.** . . . . . . . . . When it is brown underneath, **12.** . . . . . . . the pancake over and finish cooking. If you don't want to eat it immediately, **13.** . . . . . . . . it on a warm plate in the oven. **14.** . . . . . . . . with the topping of your choice.

# 35 Everyday conversations – 2

**I don't think I can do this one.**

**—Oh, come on! Have a go!**

Match each sentence on the left with the best response on the right. Use each response once only.

1. Could you spell that, please?
2. They're really friendly people, aren't they?
3. Would you like to come to the cinema with us?
4. Which of these would you like?
5. What shall we do this evening?
6. Do you want any help?
7. I'm sorry. I can't remember your surname.
8. I've passed my driving test.
9. You come from Venezuela, don't you?
10. It's very kind of you to help.
11. I don't like loud music.
12. Is it going to rain tonight?

a. How about going to the cinema?
b. It's Johnson.
c. Congratulations!
d. No, thanks. It's all right.
e. Yes, they are, aren't they?
f. Not at all.
g. I'm afraid I can't. I'm visiting my aunt.
h. The green one, please.
i. Certainly. C-U-P-B-O-A-R-D.
j. Neither do I.
k. I hope not!
l. Yes, that's right.

Write your answers here:

| 1 | 2 | 3 | 4 | 5 | 6 | 7 | 8 | 9 | 10 | 11 | 12 |
|---|---|---|---|---|---|---|---|---|----|----|----|
|   |   |   |   |   |   |   |   |   |    |    |    |

Can you think of any more responses you could give to the sentences on the left?

# 36 Sport

Choose the correct words to complete the sentences.
Look up any words you don't know.

1. This golf . . . . . . . . is one of the best in the country.
   a. court    **b.** course    c. pitch    **d.** track

2. After 5,000 metres Johnson was still . . . . . . . the lead.
   a. at    b. on    c. to    **d.** in

3. In this race they run four . . . . . . . of the track.
   **a.** laps    b. rounds    c. turns    d. courses

4. The crowd went wild when he . . . . . . . the winning goal.
   a. beat    **b.** scored    c. won    d. served

5. The surfer fell off his . . . . . . . into the waves.
   a. sledge    b. beard    **c.** board    d. paddle

6. He was . . . . . . . from the championships after they discovered he had been taking drugs.
   a. defeated    **b.** disqualified    c. lost    d. aimed

7. The champion knocked him out in the fourth . . . . . . . . . .
   **a.** round    b. part    c. game    d. challenge

8. I hope I'll be fit enough to . . . . . . . the race tomorrow.
   **a.** take part in    b. take part of    **c.** take place in    d. participate

9. An ice-. . . . . . . . match is very exciting to watch.
   a. skating    **b.** hockey    c. polo    d. puck

10. While she was serving, a string . . . . . . . in her racket.
    **a.** cut    **b.** broke    c. tore    d. blew up

11. When the . . . . . . . landed, the point stuck in the ground.
    a. discus    b. shot    c. hammer    **d.** javelin

12. They . . . . . . . gracefully over the ice.
    a. slipped    b. skidded    **c.** skated    d. rushed

13. His . . . . . . . is so fast that I can hardly see the ball.
    a. saving    b. servant    c. reservation    **d.** service

14. He had to pull out of the race with a . . . . . . . muscle.
    **a.** strained    b. cramped    c. broken    d. long

15. The . . . . . . . sped from the bow towards the target.
    a. dart    b. rod    **c.** arrow    d. bullet

16. The championships are . . . . . . . every two years.
    a. had    b. made    c. taken    **d.** held

# 37 Tools

Put the name of the tool under each picture. Choose from following list. Use each word once only.

**axe**　　　　**file**　　　　**plane**　　　**saw**
**chisel**　　**hammer**　　**pliers**　　**screwdriver**
**drill**　　　**paint brush**　**ruler**　　**spanner**

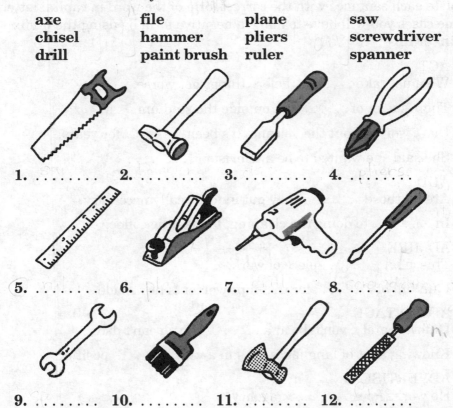

1. .......... 2. .......... 3. .......... 4. ..pliers..

5. .......... 6. .......... 7. .......... 8. ..........

9. .......... 10. .......... 11. .......... 12. ..........

Now use the best word from those above to complete each sentence.

1. I need a heavier ......... to put in this nail.
2. She got the other ......... and helped him chop the wood.
3. This ......... is the wrong size to fit around the nut.
4. He borrowed the ......... to cut the wire.
5. If you use a ......... you should get that end smooth.

47

# 38 Word formation – 1

When you look up a word in a dictionary, see if you can form any other words from it. Sometimes these words will be included in the definition of the word and sometimes they will appear separately. Look before and after each dictionary entry to see what words you can find formed from the same source.

Complete each sentence with the correct form of the word in capital letters. In some cases you will have to make a negative form by using the prefix **dis-**, **in-** or **un-**.

1. ACT
   We must take . . . . . . . . before things get worse.

   There's a lot of . . . . . . . . . . outside the stadium.

   Don't worry about the volcano. It's been . . . . . . . . for years.

   She said she wanted to be a television . . . . . . . . .

2. ADD
   Are all those . . . . . . . . they put in food really necessary?

   In . . . . . . . . to doing the cleaning, I make the coffee.

3. ADMIRE
   This is an . . . . . . . . piece of work.

   I am full of . . . . . . . for the improvements he's made.

4. ADVANTAGE
   Unfortunately, you'll be at a . . . . . . . . if you can't drive.

   Knowing a lot of languages, he's in a very . . . . . . . position.

5. ADVERTISE
   He works for an . . . . . . . . agency.

   I saw an . . . . . . . . for the job in our local newspaper.

6. AGREE
   He gets very angry if you . . . . . . . . with his ideas.

   The . . . . . . . . we made was for one year only.

7. ATTRACT
   I only had a day to visit all the tourist . . . . . . . . .

   She smiles so . . . . . . . . , doesn't she?

48

8. BASE

My grandfather only had a very . . . . . . . education.

The organisation is run on a voluntary . . . . . . . . .

9. CALCULATE

Half these . . . . . . . are wrong!

My son wants a pocket . . . . . . . . for his birthday.

He was a very cool, . . . . . . . kind of person.

10. COLLECT

Stamp . . . . . . . . can be a very expensive hobby.

Here's a special offer to all . . . . . . . . of foreign coins!

The . . . . . . . . was very successful. It raised £3,500.

11. COMPARE

I'm just a beginner in . . . . . . . . with her.

Crimes of violence were . . . . . . . rare until a few years ago.

What happened two years ago is not really . . . . . . . . to the situation now.

12. COMPETE

Would all . . . . . . . . please make their way to the start?

We're selling these toys at a very . . . . . . . . price.

If I win this . . . . . . . . , I'll get a new bicycle.

13. CONFIRM

She received a letter of . . . . . . . . from the hotel.

We've received an . . . . . . . . report of an explosion outside the President's house.

14. CONTINUE

His latest book is a . . . . . . . . of his previous one.

The train service was . . . . . . . . because it wasn't used by many people.

I couldn't get much work done as I was . . . . . . . . being interrupted by people telephoning me.

After four hours' . . . . . . . . typing I had a terrible headache.

# 39 Word partnerships – 3

Match the verb on the left with a noun on the right. Use each word once only. Write your answers in the boxes.

## Set 1

| | | | | |
|---|---|---|---|---|
| 1. bounce | a. a ball | | 1 | |
| 2. build | b. a car | | 2 | |
| 3. develop | c. coffee | | 3 | |
| 4. fold up | d. a film | | 4 | |
| 5. lick | e. an ice-cream | | 5 | |
| 6. make | f. a passport | | 6 | |
| 7. park | g. a present | | 7 | |
| 8. renew | h. a problem | | 8 | |
| 9. solve | i. an umbrella | | 9 | |
| 10. wrap | j. vocabulary | | 10 | |

## Set 2

Now do the same with these words.

| | | | | |
|---|---|---|---|---|
| 1. board | a. your ankle | | 1 | |
| 2. earn | b. a bell | | 2 | |
| 3. fire | c. a case | | 3 | |
| 4. grind | d. coffee | | 4 | |
| 5. obey | e. a coin | | 5 | g |
| 6. ring | f. a gun | | 6 | |
| 7. sprain | g. instructions | | 7 | |
| 8. tame | h. a lion | | 8 | h |
| 9. toss | i. a living | | 9 | |
| 10. unpack | j. a plane | | 10 | |

50

# 40 A pile of rubbish

When we talk about thieves, we can use the expression

a gang of thieves

There are other expressions like this and it is a good idea to note them and to learn how to use them correctly.

With the word rubbish for example, the usual expression is:

a pile of rubbish

Match the words on the left with the words on the right. Use each word once only. Write your answers in the boxes.
You will find that sometimes more than one combination is possible.
However, you should be able to find **common** combinations so that you use each word once.

| | | | | | |
|---|---|---|---|---|---|
| 1. | a block of | a. | cards | 1 | |
| 2. | a bunch of | b. | drawers | 2 | |
| 3. | a chain of | c. | false teeth | 3 | |
| 4. | a chest of | d. | flats | 4 | |
| 5. | a fleet of | e. | flowers | 5 | |
| 6. | a flock of | f. | footballers | 6 | |
| 7. | a pair of | g. | Indians | 7 | |
| 8. | a pack of | h. | potatoes | 8 | |
| 9. | a sack of | i. | sheep | 9 | |
| 10. | a set of | j. | ships | 10 | |
| 11. | a team of | k. | shops | 11 | |
| 12. | a tribe of | l. | trainers | 12 | |

Label these three correctly:

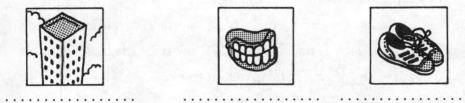

. . . . . . . . . . . . . . . . . . . .    . . . . . . . . . . . . . . . . . . .    . . . . . . . . . . . . . . . . . . .

Can you think of any more expressions using the words on the left?

# 41 'Go' and 'take'

These sentences show some of the ways in which the word 'go' can be used.
Complete each sentence by using one of the words below and part of the
verb **go** (go, goes, gone, went). Use each of these words once only.

| | | | |
|---|---|---|---|
| **ahead** | **off** | **out** | **up** |
| **grey** | **on** | **together** | **with** |

1. Having children made her hair . . . . . . . . . . . . . . . . . .
2. He . . . . . . . . . . . . . . . . about his new car all the time!
3. She . . . . . . . . . . . . . . . to the cinema last night.
4. The bomb . . . . . . . . . . . . . . . when he rang the bell.
5. That skirt . . . . . . . . very well . . . . . . . . your blouse.
6. We have permission to . . . . . . . . . . . . . . with the plan.
7. I see the price of bread has . . . . . . . . . . . . . . again.
8. These two colours don't really . . . . . . . . . . . . . . . .

Now do the same with the following words to complete sentences showing
different uses of the word 'take'.

| | | | | |
|---|---|---|---|---|
| **after** | **chance** | **out** | **medicine** | **seriously** |
| **back** | **off** | **over** | **place** | **time** |

9. The meeting will now . . . . . . . . . . . . . . . . at 10 o'clock.
10. The radio didn't work so I . . . . . . . . it . . . . . . . . to the shop.
11. . . . . . . . . your . . . . . . . . or you won't get better.
12. She . . . . . . . . . . . . . . her father; everybody says how alike they
    are!
13. The plane . . . . . . . . . . . . . . . half an hour late yesterday.
14. The dentist had to . . . . . . . . the tooth . . . . . . . . . .
15. When Ann left the company, I . . . . . . . . . . . . . . . her job.
16. They don't . . . . . . . . me . . . . . . . . . They treat me like a child.
17. I'll . . . . . . . . a . . . . . . . . and give him the job.
18. There's no hurry. . . . . . *Take* . . . your . . *time* . .

# 42 Opposites – 3

Remember that the opposite of a word depends on its context. That is why it is important to learn a word in a sentence.

What do you think the opposite of 'strong' is? One possible answer is 'weak' but, as you will see in this exercise, there are other possibilities.

Complete each sentence with the opposite of the word in brackets. Choose from one of the following words. Use each word once only.

| | | | |
|---|---|---|---|
| artificial | exact | minor | shabby |
| compulsory | faint | partial | stale |
| considerable | flexible | positive | strong |
| even | hollow | rough | tough |

1.  I can give you the . . . . . . . . figures now. (APPROXIMATE)

2.  The sea was very . . . . . . . . that day. (CALM)

3.  The operation was a . . . . . . . . success. (COMPLETE)

4.  I put the . . . . . . . . bread in the cupboard. (FRESH)

5.  He's in hospital for a . . . . . . . . operation. (MAJOR)

6.  Is this one a . . . . . . . . curry? (MILD)

7.  He always wore very . . . . . . . . clothes. (NEAT)

8.  She has a . . . . . . . . influence on the boy. (NEGATIVE)

9.  The houses with . . . . . . . . numbers are on this side. (ODD)

10. Are the flowers in that window . . . . . . . . ? (REAL)

11. There's a . . . . . . . . difference between the two. (SLIGHT)

12. The figure was holding a large . . . . . . . . ball. (SOLID)

13. It was made of some kind of . . . . . . . . material. (STIFF)

14. There's a . . . . . . . . smell of gas in the kitchen. (STRONG)

15. My steak was very . . . . . . . . . (TENDER)

16. Playing football is . . . . . . . . at this school. (VOLUNTARY)

# 43 -able or -ible?

Complete the adjectives in each set by using the correct letter.
In addition, form the opposite by using the correct prefix. The prefix will
be one of the following:

**il-, im-, in-, ir-** or **un-**

Finally, match the adjective formed with a suitable noun. Use each word
once only. Write your answer in the space provided.

## Set 1

un avoid a ble          . . . . . . . . . . . . . . . .          accident

comfort ble          . . . . . . . . . . . . . .          behaviour

im ed ble amenable    . . *Uncomfortable* . .          chair

un favour ble          . . . . . . . . . . . . . . . .          food

im respons ble          . . . . . . . . . . . . . .          report

## Set 2

un break ble          . . . . . . . . . . . . . .          china

im read ble          . . . . . . . . . . . . . . . .          decision

in reli ble          . . . . . . . . . . . . . . . .          novel

revers ble          . . . . . . . . . . . . . . . .          weather

un season ble          . . . . . . . . . . . . . .          witness

## Set 3

ir digest ble          . . . . . . . . . . . . . . . .          attitude

in cur ble          . . . . . . . . . . . . . . . .          explanation

un flex ble          . . . . . . . . . . . . . . . .          food

il leg ble          . . . . . . . . . . . . . . . .          handwriting

un prob ble          . . . . . . . . . . . . . .          illness

# 44 Horrible joke time

Different people find different things funny.
Here are some examples of jokes which some people find quite amusing.
(Other people think they are just silly.)
Match the question on the left with the answer on the right.

| | | | |
|---|---|---|---|
| **1.** | What is at the end of everything? | **a.** | Her husband. |
| **2.** | How do you stop food from going bad? | **b.** | Baby elephants. |
| **3.** | Which word is always pronounced wrongly? | **c.** | Two — the inside and the outside. |
| **4.** | If a man married a princess, what would he be? | **d.** | Darling, of course I do! |
| **5.** | Where does a large gorilla sit when it goes to the theatre? | **e.** | Time to get a new one. |
| **6.** | Excuse me. Do you know the quickest way to the station? | **f.** | A noise. |
| **7.** | If your clock strikes thirteen, what time is it? | **g.** | The letter 'g'. |
| **8.** | What can you make but can't see? | **h.** | A table. |
| **9.** | How many sides has a box got? | **i.** | Yes. Take a taxi. |
| **10.** | What's your new dog's name? | **j.** | Paint. |
| **11.** | What do elephants have that no other animal has? | **k.** | By eating it. |
| **12.** | What's the best thing to put in a fruit cake? | **l.** | Anywhere it wants to. |
| **13.** | What has legs but can't walk? | **m.** | WRONGLY. |
| **14.** | Will you still love me when I'm not beautiful any more? | **n.** | I don't know. He won't tell me. |
| **15.** | What do you put on when it's wet? | **o.** | Your teeth. |

Write your answers here:

| 1 | 2 | 3 | 4 | 5 | 6 | 7 | 8 | 9 | 10 | 11 | 12 | 13 | 14 | 15 |
|---|---|---|---|---|---|---|---|---|----|----|----|----|----|----|
|   |   |   |   |   |   |   |   |   |    |    |    |    |    |    |

# 45 Guess the ending

Predicting — guessing what comes next — helps you to listen and read more effectively.

Find some sentences in this or another of your English books. Cover the final word or words and see if you can guess what they are. Maybe you will think of a different way to end the sentence. That doesn't matter. The important thing is to learn how words go together.

Complete the following sentences with one word only.

1. I've just borrowed these books from the local . . . . . . . . . .
2. I can't stir my tea. They haven't given me a . . . . . . . . .
3. The car stopped because they had run out of . . . . . . . . . .
4. Before we go shopping I'll go to the bank and get some more . . . . .
5. Look up any word you don't understand in your . . . . . . . . . .
6. Dinner will be ready in a minute. I've just got to lay the . . . . . . . .
7. Her eyesight is so bad that she wears special . . . . . . . . .
8. Mary! Get a handkerchief and blow your . . . . . . . . !
9. I wish he wouldn't ask such embarrassing . . . . . . . . !
10. A game of football isn't over until the referee blows his . . . . . . . . .
11. He's a terrible cook. He can't even boil an . . . . . . . . !
12. They say this new plane is much easier to . . . . . . . . .
13. I can't cut this paper. I need some sharper . . . . . . . . .
14. Please put these names in alphabetical . . . . . . . .
15. She added more water because the soup was too . . . . . . . . . .
16. Do this homework again! You've made a lot of silly . . . . . . . .

56

# 46 Phrasal verbs – 2

By matching the numbers with the letters find the phrasal verbs with the meanings given.

| | | | | | |
|---|---|---|---|---|---|
| 1 LOOK | | 2 RUN | | 3 TURN |
| | 4 SET | | 5 SLIP | |
| 6 TAKE | | 7 CARRY | | 8 PUT |
| | 9 GO | | 10 GET | |
| A AWAY | | B INTO | | C AFTER |
| | D UP | | E DOWN | |
| F BY | | G OUT | | H THROUGH |
| | I ON | | J OFF | |

| | | |
|---|---|---|
| BE SIMILAR TO | 6 | C |
| CONTINUE | 7 | I |
| ESCAPE | 2 | a |
| EXPERIENCE | 9 | H |
| EXTINGUISH | 8 | g |
| INVESTIGATE | 1 | B |
| MAKE A MISTAKE | 5 | d |
| MANAGE | 10 | F |
| REJECT | 3 | e |
| START A JOURNEY | 4 | J |

Use the phrasal verbs to complete each of these sentences:

1. If you're finding it difficult to ..... get by ..... on your salary, why don't you ask for a rise?
2. I know what you're going through ... and I feel really sorry for you.
3. In many ways you ... take after ... your father.
4. If you .. slip up ......, you'll get into trouble.
5. I proposed to her but she .. turned me ... down .
6. You'd better ... put out ..... your cigarette because smoking isn't allowed in here.
7. If you .... carry on ... working so hard, you'll make yourself ill.
8. The advantage of ... set off ..... early is that you'll be able to miss all the traffic.
9. Don't run away ....! I don't want to borrow anything; I just want a quick word with you.
10. The manager promised to .. look into .... the matter in response to my letter.

57

# 47 Word formation – 2

Complete each sentence with the correct form of the word in capital letters. In some cases you will have to make a negative form by using the prefix **in-** or **un-**.

**1.**    CONVENIENCE

I'm afraid it won't be . . . . . . . . for me to see you tomorrow.

The house is . . . . . . . . situated near the centre of town.

This is very . . . . . . . . ! Can't you practise your violin somewhere else?

**2.**    CREATE

I would like to show you my latest . . . . . . . . , which I have called 'Boats on a Lake'.

The chameleon is a very strange . . . . . . . . . .

Conan Doyle was famous as the . . . . . . . . of the great detective, Sherlock Holmes.

**3.**    CRITIC

Why does everybody . . . . . . . . him all the time?

After so much . . . . . . . . he felt he had to resign.

They were very . . . . . . . . of his efforts to improve services.

**4.**    DECIDE

They're going to announce their . . . . . . . . tomorrow.

He's so . . . . . . . . ! He just can't make up his mind!

**5.**    DECORATE

The . . . . . . . . said he would charge me £1,000 a room.

During the festival . . . . . . . . were hanging from every tree.

**6.**    DEMONSTRATE

The . . . . . . . . all sat down in the middle of the road.

He offered to give me a . . . . . . . . of how the machine worked.

**7.    DEPEND**

We are . . . . . . . . on other countries for most of our food.

Every year we celebrate our . . . . . . . . .

**8.    DICTATE**

The boss wants you to take some . . . . . . . . . .

He acted in an extremely . . . . . . . manner, which made him very unpopular.

**9.    DIRECT**

Are you sure we're going in the right . . . . . . . . ?

She looked . . . . . . . . at me as she said it.

I had to look up the number in the telephone . . . . . . . . . .

Hitchcock is one of my favourite film . . . . . . . . .

**10.    ECONOMY**

My new car is more . . . . . . . than the one I had before.

She studied . . . . . . . at university.

On my salary we have to live as . . . . . . . . as possible.

If we don't . . . . . . . . on electricity, there will be power cuts.

**11.    ELECTRIC**

He works as an . . . . . . . . for a local firm.

The price of . . . . . . . has gone up again.

The fire was caused by an . . . . . . . . fault in the television.

He is an . . . . . . . . engineer.

**12.    EMPLOY**

Last December the boss gave all his . . . . . . . . a bonus.

I've been . . . . . . . . since June. I must find work soon.

Her . . . . . . . . was so angry at her attitude that he fired her.

He hoped the . . . . . . . . agency would find him a job.

**13.    ENTHUSIASM**

They all cheered . . . . . . . . as their team came out.

I'm afraid they weren't very . . . . . . . . about your idea of going out this evening.

# 48 Health – 2

Choose the best alternative to complete the sentence.
Look up any words you don't know.

1. A bone got stuck in her throat and she started . . . . . . . . .
   a. strangling  b. choking  c. sniffing  d. suffocating

2. The doctor gave me an . . . . . . . . to relieve the pain.
   a. infection  b. invalid  c. injection  d. epidemic

3. I'm . . . . . . . . tomatoes. They bring me out in a rash.
   a. allergic to  b. polluted by  c. wounded by  d. suffering from

4. She had lost so much blood that they gave her a . . . . . . . . .
   a. circulation  b. transplant  c. resuscitation  d. transfusion

5. It took me weeks to . . . . . . . . my illness.
   a. recover from  b. lessen  c. soothe  d. neglect

6. His . . . . . . . . was so bad that he never used a lift.
   a. agoraphobia  b. claustrophobia  c. insomnia  d. antidote

7. A course of . . . . . . . . got rid of the pains in his back.
   a. physiotherapy  b. casualty  c. anatomy  d. veterinary

8. After his heart . . . . . . . . he was told to relax more.
   a. attack  b. turn  c. ache  d. diet

9. The . . . . . . . . operated on his appendix.
   a. chiropodist  b. midwife  c. surgeon  d. pharmacist

10. She's . . . . . . . . from a nervous breakdown.
    a. healing  b. fainting  c. suffering  d. itching

11. There was an . . . . . . . . of cholera after the disaster.
    a. upset  b. infection  c. input  d. outbreak

12. Her broken arm will be in . . . . . . . . for another week.
    a. plaster  b. fracture  c. joint  d. fever

13. I had trouble getting that . . . . . . . . out of my finger.
    a. splint  b. splinter  c. sponge  d. spasm

14. He had an uncontrollable . . . . . . . . caused by tiredness.
    a. stretch  b. scratch  c. twist  d. twitch

15. The instruments were . . . . . . . . before the operation.
    a. sterilized  b. disinfected  c. diagnosed  d. immunized

16. When the doctor arrived, he found that her husband had
    already . . . . . . . . the baby himself.
    a. delivered  b. controlled  c. pulled  d. passed out

60

# 49 Expressions with 'would'

Each of these conversations includes an expression with 'would' or 'd'.
Complete them with the words below:

**shame rather nice   time   point waste admit**
**same  first mind  silly   never  fair  surprise**

1.  "Do you fancy a drink?"
    "That'd be . . *nice* . . ."

2.  "Couldn't we meet them on our way to the airport?"
    "There wouldn't be . . *time* . . ."

3.  "We've been working for three hours now. Would you like a
    break?"
    "I wouldn't . *mind* . . ."

4.  "If it rains, they'll have to cancel the whole thing."
    "That'd be a . . *shame* ."

5.  "I know he's been training very hard, but don't you think we
    should choose someone else for the team?"
    "No, that wouldn't be . . . . *fair* ."

6.  "I might take a few days holiday while I'm in Vienna for the
    conference."
    "Good idea. You'd be . *silly* . . not to."

7.  "I know she's refused you once, but you could ask her out again."
    "No, there wouldn't be any . . *point* . ."

8.  "She's always late. I bet she's late again this time."
    "It wouldn't *surprise* me."

9.  "It's a pity your college friends can't come, but can't we go ahead
    with the party anyway?"
    "No, it just wouldn't be the . *same* . ."

10. "He seems confident, but apparently he gets quite nervous."
    "You'd *never* . know!"

11. "Why not ask your father to lend you the money? He's not that
    mean, is he?"
    "I'm afraid he is. It'd be a . *waste* . of time."

12. "He'll probably blame the whole thing on you."
    "It wouldn't be the . *first* . . time."

13. "I think you upset them."
    "Well, I am a bit blunt, I know. I'd be the first to *admit* it. But
    they were asking for it!"

14. "Shall we go out for a meal this evening?"
    "I'm a bit tired actually. I'd . . . . . . . . . not, if you don't mind."
    *rather*

61

# 50 Money – 2

Choose the correct word to complete the sentence.
Look up any words you don't know.

1. If business has been good, the staff get a . . . . . . . . at the end of the year.
   **a.** notice    **b.** bonus    **c.** fund    **d.** deposit

2. He drew all his money . . . . . . . . the bank before he left.
   **a.** of    **b.** off    **c.** out of    **d.** to

3. Where can I get a good rate of . . . . . . . . for my money?
   **a.** credit    **b.** interest    **c.** debt    **d.** bargain

4. We'll have to economise . . . . . . . . luxuries in the future.
   **a.** for    **b.** at    **c.** of    **d.** on

5. They want to get young people to open a bank . . . . . . . . .
   **a.** count    **b.** account    **c.** counter    **d.** deposit

6. Could you give me an . . . . . . . . of how much it will cost?
   **a.** income    **b.** estimate    **c.** invoice    **d.** expenditure

7. You have to pay a . . . . . . . . now to reserve your holiday.
   **a.** deposit    **b.** security    **c.** credit    **d.** surplus

8. As the car is small, it's much more . . . . . . . . on petrol.
   **a.** expensive    **b.** poor    **c.** economical    **d.** economic

9. All employees had to cut down on travelling . . . . . . . . . .
   **a.** expenses    **b.** savings    **c.** stoppages    **d.** wages

10. My credit card is . . . . . . . . in most countries.
    **a.** exchanged    **b.** reserved    **c.** excepted    **d.** accepted

11. The bill came . . . . . . . . $100.
    **a.** at    **b.** for    **c.** to    **d.** as

12. They . . . . . . . . part of his wages for being late.
    **a.** reduced    **b.** deduced    **c.** deducted    **d.** retired

13. Could you lend me £20? I'm a bit short . . . . . . . . money.
    **a.** of    **b.** off    **c.** with    **d.** from

14. They persuaded him to . . . . . . . . money in their company.
    **a.** investigate    **b.** buy    **c.** invest    **d.** lay

15. You'll get a better . . . . . . . . of exchange at a bank.
    **a.** rate    **b.** value    **c.** worth    **d.** charge

16. The meals are such a reasonable price because they are . . . . . . . . by the company.
    **a.** allowed    **b.** reduced    **c.** deducted    **d.** subsidized

# 51 In a bookshop

Learn more words by thinking of the things you see and use every day. Do you know their names in English?

Think about the books you may have at home. Do you know what type of book you would call each one? After you have done this exercise, see if you can categorize any books or magazines you have.

Below you will see a plan of one of the floors of a bookshop. You have to decide in which section you would expect to find each of the following books. You must use each section once only in your answers.

1. Beethoven's Symphonies
2. Black and White Developing
3. Cake-Making Can Be Fun
4. Car Maintenance Made Easy
5. First Aid at Home
6. Improve Your Tennis
7. Life in Roman Times
8. Looking After Your Lawn
9. Love in the Clouds
10. Murder in the Afternoon
11. The Paintings of Turner
12. Socialism Today
13. Wall-Papering Made Easy
14. Webster's Dictionary
15. Western Movies
16. Where to go in Paris

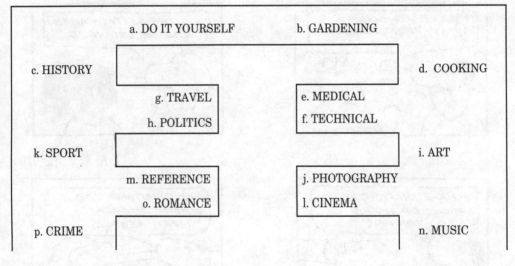

a. DO IT YOURSELF    b. GARDENING

c. HISTORY    d. COOKING

g. TRAVEL    e. MEDICAL
h. POLITICS    f. TECHNICAL

k. SPORT    i. ART

m. REFERENCE    j. PHOTOGRAPHY
o. ROMANCE    l. CINEMA

p. CRIME    n. MUSIC

Write your answers here:

| 1 | 2 | 3 | 4 | 5 | 6 | 7 | 8 | 9 | 10 | 11 | 12 | 13 | 14 | 15 | 16 |
|---|---|---|---|---|---|---|---|---|----|----|----|----|----|----|----|
| n | j | d | f | e | k | c | b | o | p  | c  | c  | a  | c  | a  | d  |

# 52 Problems, problems

I have difficulty
waking up in the morning.
— If I were you, I'd
go to bed earlier.

Match each sentence below with the best response on the next page. Use each response once only.

**I'M NOT CERTAIN WHAT TIME THE TRAIN LEAVES.**

1. . . . . . . . . . . . . . . . . . . . . .

**I WANT A HOLIDAY AWAY FROM ALL THE CROWDS.**

3. . . . . . . . . . . . . . . . . . . . .

**I HAVE DIFFICULTY WAKING UP IN THE MORNING.**

5. . . . . . . . . . . . . . . . . . . . .

**THIS PLAY IS REALLY BORING.**

2. . . . . . . . . . . . . . . . . . . . .

**ALL THE RESTAURANTS WILL BE CROWDED.**

4. . . . . . . . . . . . . . . . . . .

**SHE WANTS A JOB WHERE SHE CAN MEET PEOPLE.**

6. . . . . . . . . . . . . . . . . . . . .

7. ........J.........

8. ........K.........

9. ........d.........

10. ........f.........

11. ........J.........

12. ........C.........

a. You'd better ring the station, then.
b. Let's leave during the interval.
c. They say that new shampoo's very good.
d. Why don't you ask him to turn it down?
e. Why not try it on, sir?
f. We can take a picnic if you like.

g. Well, maybe she could try working in a hotel.
h. How about a bicycle?
i. All right. Let's rent a cottage in the country.
j. What about apple juice?
k. You shouldn't stay out in the sun so long.
l. If I were you, I'd go to bed earlier.

Can you think of any more responses you could give to the sentences in the cartoons?

# 53 Using a trade directory

In a trade directory, services and suppliers are listed under appropriate headings.

In this exercise you have to decide which heading from the following list you would look under for what you need. Use each heading once only. Write your answers in the boxes.

1. **CAR BODY REPAIRS**
2. **CHIROPODISTS**
3. **ESTATE AGENTS**
4. **FURNITURE REPAIRS**
5. **GLAZIERS**
6. **LAUNDRIES**
7. **LOCKSMITHS**
8. **OFFICE EQUIPMENT**
9. **OPTICIANS**
10. **PET SHOPS**
11. **SOLARIUMS**
12. **TAILORS**
13. **TAXIS**
14. **TRANSLATORS**
15. **TRAVEL AGENTS**

## PROBLEM

a. Your armchair is broken.

b. You need a duplicate key.

c. Your suit is too tight.

d. You want to sell your house.

e. You want to be driven to the station.

f. You want to buy a cat.

g. You've driven into a wall.

h. Your typewriter is broken.

i. Your feet keep hurting.

j. You want a suntan before your holiday.

k. You've got a lot of dirty shirts.

l. You've received a letter in Russian.

m. You need a holiday.

n. Your glasses are broken.

o. Somebody has broken one of your windows.

| | |
|----|----|
| 1 | g |
| 2 | i |
| 3 | d |
| 4 | a |
| 5 | o |
| 6 | k |
| 7 | b |
| 8 | h |
| 9 | n |
| 10 | f |
| 11 | j |
| 12 | c |
| 13 | e |
| 14 | l |
| 15 | m |

Look again at page 13. Cover the words at the top of the page. Look at the pictures for one minute. Now write down as many of the words as you can remember without looking at the pictures again. Remember, looking back and revising what you have already learned is an important part of building your vocabulary.

# 54 Stress patterns

When you look up a word in the dictionary, you should make sure you know how to pronounce it. One problem is knowing where the stress is. Your dictionary should show you this.

If you stress a word wrongly, it makes you very difficult to understand. Stress is often more important than perfect pronunciation.

In this exercise you must put each of the words below into the correct list depending on its stress pattern.
The sign ▼ shows the main stress.
The first word is shown as an example.

| | | | |
|---|---|---|---|
| advertise | character | expensive | operator |
| advertisement | departure | indication | receptionist |
| advertising | disagree | indicator | sensible |
| assistant | disagreement | lemonade | understanding |
| bachelor | discussion | mispronounce | understatement |
| biography | disqualify | operation | unemployed |

**1.** ▼○○

*advertise*

..........................
..........................
..........................
..........................

**2.** ○▼○

..........................
..........................
..........................
..........................

**3.** ○○▼

..........................
..........................
..........................
..........................

**4.** ▼○○○

..........................
..........................
..........................
..........................

**5.** ○▼○○

..........................
..........................
..........................
..........................

**6.** ○○▼○

..........................
..........................
..........................
..........................

# 55 Education

Don't forget to keep choosing topics and to make lists of vocabulary for them. Test yourself by thinking of a topic and seeing how many words you can write down (spelled correctly of course). Before you do this exercise, see how many words you know on the topic of education.

Complete each sentence by using a word from the list.
Use each word once only.

| | | |
|---|---|---|
| attend | mark | subject |
| enrol | playground | syllabus |
| examination | principal | term |
| gymnasium | pupil | timetable |
| homework | staff | uniform |

1. Her teacher sent her to talk to the principal as her work was so bad.

2. There are 25 members of . staff . . in our school.

3. If you work hard, you should pass the . examination

4. He had to teach everything on the subject . . before the end of the year. syllabus

5. You get a diploma if you . attend . . the classes regularly.

6. If it rains, we'll play the game in the . gymnasium

7. The highest . mark . . was eighteen out of twenty.

8. I have so much . home . . . that I can't come out tonight. work

9. You can . enrol . . . for these courses next week.

10. She left school before the end of the summer . . term . . .

11. On the timetable . it says he teaches class 2B at midday.

12. I think French is my favourite . subject . .

13. At my school everybody has to wear the same . uniform . .

14. She was the best . pupil . . . in the class.

15. As it's raining they can't go outside in the . playground

# 56 Confusing words – 2

Some dictionaries give examples of English words which are commonly confused. If you have difficulty choosing the correct word, look in your dictionary to see if there are examples of the right word and the wrong word used correctly in sentences. Try to write **your own** sentences so that you can remember how to use the words correctly.

Choose the correct alternative from each pair.

## Set 1

My boss **1. said/told** that unless I **2. raised/rose** the standard of my work, I was likely to **3. loose/lose** my job. With the cost of **4. life/living** rising all the time, the consequences would be disastrous. As it is, I'm finding it **5. almost/hardly** impossible to make ends meet on my monthly **6. salary/wage**. This morning I **7. lost/missed** the bus to the office and I turned up late again. My boss **8. said/told** me that if the same situation **9. arose/aroused** again, he would have no choice but to give me the sack. I couldn't bear being out of work as I'm used to having a **10. stable/steady** job. The problem is that I'm not in the **11. custom/habit** of getting up early as I used to start work **12. later/lately**. It's not easy to find a **13. job/work** in the **14. actual/present 15. economic/economical 16. climate/condition**. And, of course things are getting more difficult for me; the **17. elder/older** you get, the more difficult it is to find any job, never mind one which **18. gives/pays** a reasonable wage.

## Set 2

If you have a **1. flair/flare** for languages, don't **2. lose/waste** the **3. opportunity/possibility** of studying in the country where the language is spoken. **4. As far as/As long as** you're prepared to be patient, you'll find the experience invaluable. **5. However/Moreover,** there's no point in taking such a step unless you use your time well. You can't expect to learn a language overnight so don't **6. raise/rise** your hopes too high. As a rule, the more advanced you are, the slower you seem to **7. do/make** headway. You should also **8. bare/bear** in mind the fact that what you do outside the classroom is likely to **9. affect/effect** your progress. As you'll only **10. pass/spend** a short period of each day in school, it helps if you can make **11. friend/friends** with native speakers so that you have the chance to practise. Another useful tip is to **12. look at/watch** television and listen to the radio. There are plenty of opportunities and if you are prepared to work hard you will certainly get a lot out of the experience.

# 57 Emphasis

Sometimes you want to be able to say something in a stronger way.
Complete the dialogues below using one of the following strong
adjectives:

| | | | | |
|---|---|---|---|---|
| enormous | gorgeous | impossible | fantastic | boiling |
| fascinating | delicious | spotless | freezing | minute |
| hideous | tedious | charming | disgusting | filthy |

1. "Was it a good hotel?"
   "Good? It was absolutely ..fantastic......!"
2. "Was it a big place?"
   "Big? It was absolutely ...enormous.....!"
3. "Was it a small room?"
   "Small? It was absolutely ...minute.......!"
4. "Was it hot in Seville?"
   "Hot? It was absolutely ...boiling.......!"
5. "Was it cold in Helsinki?"
   "Cold? It was absolutely ...freezing.......!"
6. "Was she as beautiful as they say?"
   "Beautiful? She was absolutely ...gorgeous.....!" *fascinating*
7. "Was the dining-room as ugly as the lounge?"
   "Ugly? It was absolutely ...disgusting..hideous..!"
8. "Was the house clean?"
   "Clean? It was absolutely ...spotless.......!"
9. "Was the beach dirty?"
   "Dirty? It was absolutely ....filthy.......!"
10. "Was it an interesting place?"
    "Interesting? It was absolutely .fascinating....!"
11. "Wasn't it a bit boring?"
    "Boring? It was absolutely ...tedious.......!"
12. "Was the exam difficult?"
    "Difficult? It was absolutely ..impossible.....!"
13. "Was she nice?"
    "Nice? She was absolutely ...charming.......!"
14. "Was the steak as good as it looked?"
    "Good? It was absolutely ....delicious......!"
15. "Was the food in the hotel as bad as last year?"
    "Bad? It was absolutely ...disgusting.....!"

# 58 Jobs

Which of the following jobs can you see in the picture below? Write your list under the picture.

| | | | |
|---|---|---|---|
| **bank clerk** | **docker** | **nurse** | **priest** |
| **bus conductor** | **dustman** | **optician** | **secretary** |
| **bus driver** | **electrician** | **plumber** | **traffic warden** |
| **cashier** | **florist** | **policeman** | **waitress** |
| **dentist** | **miner** | **postman** | **window cleaner** |

bus conductor ........ bank clerk ........ bus driver
cashier ........ dentist ........ dustman
electrician ........ nurse ........ plumber
policeman ........ postman ........ priest
secretary ........ traffic ........ warden
........ cleaner

# 59 Word formation and partnerships

Some verbs can be formed by adding **-en**, **-ify** or **-ise** (sometimes spelled **-ize**) to an adjective or noun.
Sometimes changes in spelling are necessary, for example:

| | |
|---|---|
| fat | fatten (a lamb) |
| mystery | mystify (an audience) |
| authority | authorise (entry) |

Form a verb from the noun or adjective on the left and write it in the space provided. Next match the verb you have formed with an appropriate noun on the right. Use each word once only. Write your answers in the boxes.

## Set 1

1. computer _computerise_      **a.** a kitchen
2. emphasis _emphasize_      **b.** a point
3. identity _identify_      **c.** a road
4. memory _memorise_      **d.** a skirt
5. modern _modernise_      **e.** the soup
6. pure _purify_      **f.** a system
7. short _shorten_      **g.** a telephone number
8. thick _thicken_      **h.** a thief
9. wide _widen_      **i.** water

| | |
|---|---|
| 1 | f |
| 2 | b |
| 3 | h |
| 4 | g |
| 5 | a |
| 6 | i |
| 7 | d |
| 8 | e |
| 9 | c |

## Set 2

1. apology _apologize_      **a.** books
2. bright _brighten_      **b.** butter
3. class _classify_      **c.** a collar
4. loose _loosen_      **d.** a knife
5. sharp _sharpen_      **e.** for a mistake
6. soft _soften_      **f.** muscles
7. special _specialise_      **g.** a room
8. strength _strengthen_      **h.** in sports cars
9. terror _terrorize_      **i.** victims

| | |
|---|---|
| 1 | e |
| 2 | g |
| 3 | a |
| 4 | c |
| 5 | d |
| 6 | b |
| 7 | m |
| 8 | f |
| 9 | i |

72

# 60 Sounds and movements

Keep looking at what is happening around you and ask yourself if you know how to describe it in English. Before you do this exercise, see how many verbs you can list describing sounds and then do the same for verbs describing movements. After you have done the exercise add any new words you have learnt to your lists.

Below you will see some verbs which either describe sounds or movements. You have to put each verb in the correct list.

| | | | |
|---|---|---|---|
| bend | hop | shake | snatch |
| climb | hum | shout | stammer |
| creep | jump | shrug | talk |
| cry | lift | sing | wander |
| giggle | mumble | slide | whisper |
| groan | scream | slip | whistle |

## 1. SOUNDS

. . . . . . . . . . . . . . . . . . . . . . . . .
. . . . . . . . . . . . . . . . . . . . . . . . .
. . . . . . . . . . . . . . . . . . . . . . . . .
. . . . . . . . . . . . . . . . . . . . . . . . .
. . . . . . . . . . . . . . . . . . . . . . . . .
. . . . . . . . . . . . . . . . . . . . . . . . .
. . . . . . . . . . . . . . . . . . . . . . . . .
. . . . . . . . . . . . . . . . . . . . . . . . .
. . . . . . . . . . . . . . . . . . . . . . . . .
. . . . . . . . . . . . . . . . . . . . . . . . .
. . . . . . . . . . . . . . . . . . . . . . . . .

## 2. MOVEMENTS

. . . . . . . . . . . . . . . . . . . . . . . . .
. . . . . . . . . . . . . . . . . . . . . . . . .
. . . . . . . . . . . . . . . . . . . . . . . . .
. . . . . . . . . . . . . . . . . . . . . . . . .
. . . . . . . . . . . . . . . . . . . . . . . . .
. . . . . . . . . . . . . . . . . . . . . . . . .
. . . . . . . . . . . . . . . . . . . . . . . . .
. . . . . . . . . . . . . . . . . . . . . . . . .
. . . . . . . . . . . . . . . . . . . . . . . . .
. . . . . . . . . . . . . . . . . . . . . . . . .

Remember to keep adding new words to your lists as you meet them.

# 61 Word formation – 3

Remember to keep looking for words which are formed from the same source. Make lists of these words and test yourself. As a start, look at the words in capital letters in the word formation exercises in this book and see how many words you can form from them.

Complete each sentence with the correct form of the word in capital letters. In some cases you may have to make a negative form by using the prefix **dis-**, **in-** or **un-**.

**1.   HONEST**

It was very . . .dishonest. . . . . . of him to steal that money.

I . .honestly. . . think that this is the best thing to do.

They praised her for her . . . .honesty. . . . .

**2.   IDENTIFY**

Have you got some kind of . .identification. . . . . on you?

UFO means . . .Unidentified. . . . Flying Object.

**3.   IMAGINE**

They said my illness was . . . . . . . . . . . . . Don't they realise I'm in a lot of pain?

He hasn't got the . . . . . . . . to think up such a clever plan.

**4.   INDUSTRY**

I'm afraid . . . . . . . relations aren't very good in this company.

She was a much less . . . . . . . student than her sister.

He's a leading . . . . . . . . , with factories all over the country.

In the past few years this area has become heavily . . . . . . . . . .

**5.   MANAGE**

The . . . . . . . . said he wouldn't change the radio without a receipt.

They are taking over the . . . . . . . . of the company next week.

Only the . . . . . . . Director can make that decision.

She's got a job as the . . . . . . . . of a dress shop.

**6.  NATION**

If he isn't Spanish, what . . . . . . . . is he?

The coal industry was originally private but was . . . . . . . . in the 1940's.

There's no . . . . . . . . service in the United Kingdom.

**7.  OBSERVE**

It was very . . . . . . . . of you to notice that.

This . . . . . . . . houses the largest telescope in the country.

He's under . . . . . . . . all the time.

**8.  SATISFY**

He couldn't give a . . . . . . . . explanation for his actions.

I get no . . . . . . . . from doing this.

I'm afraid I was very . . . . . . . . with the travel arrangements.

**9.  SCIENCE**

She's a top . . . . . . . . working on our space project.

There is no . . . . . . . . explanation for what happened.

The connection hasn't been . . . . . . . . proved yet.

**10.  SHORT**

Mrs Bailey will be with you . . . . . . . . . .

I had to . . . . . . . . my speech as we had started late.

There is a . . . . . . . . of carrots because of the bad weather.

**11.  VARY**

The temperature is very . . . . . . . . at this time of year.

Do you like this new . . . . . . . . of apple?

There are . . . . . . . . desserts to choose from.

Politicians . . . . . . . . . . . . . blame the media if they don't win the election. They're so predictable.

# 62 Product information – 2

Remember that you don't have to be in an English-speaking country to see real English. It is usually possible to buy an English newspaper or magazine or even get one sent to you. The advertisements in them can be very useful in helping you build up lists of words used when talking about different products.

In this exercise you will see some information about a product. You must decide which product is being referred to. Choose the product from the following list. Each product is referred to once only.

| | | | |
|---|---|---|---|
| barbecue | camera | game | radio |
| bathroom heater | clock | iron | suitcase |
| bed | clothes line | kettle | tape recorder |
| bedside cabinet | food mixer | necklace | vacuum cleaner |

20 inch grill. Choice of four cooking positions. Comes complete with spit. Overall height 33 inch.

1. ..*barbecue*..

Thermostat control. Suitable for right or left hand use. Safety thermal cut-out.

2. ...*iron*.........

Picks up a wide range of household and workshop dirt including liquids. 900 watt. Complete with tools.

3. ...*vacuum. cleaner*..

Length 16 inch approx. 20-year guarantee on pearls.

4. ...*necklace*...

Built-in flash. Motorized film advance. Normal and telephoto lenses.

5. .....*camera*

Extends up to 15 feet giving 70 feet of drying space.

6. ...*clothes line*....

Mounted on castors. Includes headboard and 3 inch thick mattress. Size 6 ft 3 inch x 2 ft 3 inch.

7. ......... *bed* ....

Built-in microphone and earphone socket. Compatible with most home computers. 240V ac mains or 4 x R14S batteries.

8. ...... *tape recorder*

Thermostat control. Wall mounted. Safety cut-out. Pull cord operated.

9. ..... *bathroom* ..

Useful cupboard and shelf storage. Size 13 x 12 x 23 inch high approx.

10. ..... *bedside*

In 'leather-look' vinyl. Twin locks with straps and buckles. Comes complete with wheels and towing handle.

11. ...... *suitcase*

Crescendo repeat alarm. Snooze feature. Dial light.

12. ...... *clock* ..

Water level indicator. Maximum capacity 3 pint. 2000 watt.

13. .... *kettle* ....

3-speed. With detachable stand, power-driven bowl, beaters and liquidizer. 160 watt.

14. ...... *food mixer*

For 2–4 players. Ages 5 years and over.

15. .... *game* ....

Long, medium and VHF waveband coverage. Carrying handle.

16. .... *radio* ....

# 63 Business

Choose the best alternative to complete the sentence.
Look up any words you don't know.

1. I'm afraid he's away . . . . . . . business today.
   **a.** with     **b.** on     **c.** in     **d.** to

2. We also do repairs in . . . . . . . to our car-hire business.
   **a.** comparison   **b.** reply     **c.** addition     **d.** exception

3. I've applied . . . . . . . the position of sales manager.
   **a.** to     **b.** as     **c.** for     **d.** about

4. Does our insurance . . . . . . . cover accidental damage?
   **a.** policy     **b.** politics     **c.** subsidy     **d.** account

5. With . . . . . . . to your letter of 10th September, I would like to place an order for your new travel guide.
   **a.** referring     **b.** reading     **c.** reference     **d.** reception

6. The new organization consists . . . . . . . five divisions.
   **a.** in     **b.** with     **c.** on     **d.** of

7. Does the design . . . . . . . to the new regulations?
   **a.** agree     **b.** conform     **c.** confirm     **d.** consist

8. My bank has . . . . . . . in towns all over the country.
   **a.** branches     **b.** warehouses   **c.** depots     **d.** head offices

9. He was dismissed . . . . . . . giving away trade secrets.
   **a.** for     **b.** with     **c.** by     **d.** to

10. Could I have a secretary to take some . . . . . . . ?
    **a.** writing     **b.** dictating     **c.** dictation     **d.** commission

11. She put . . . . . . . an interesting proposal.
    **a.** to     **b.** against     **c.** forward     **d.** backwards

12. Could the manager . . . . . . . with this enquiry?
    **a.** trade     **b.** see     **c.** talk     **d.** deal

13. We have pleasure . . . . . . . enclosing our latest brochure.
    **a.** to     **b.** in     **c.** for     **d.** with

14. She . . . . . . . because she had been offered a better job.
    **a.** resigned     **b.** sacked     **c.** fired     **d.** dismissed

15. The agreement will . . . . . . . trade between our countries.
    **a.** increase     **b.** inflate     **c.** add up     **d.** exaggerate

16. Please do not . . . . . . . to contact our office in case of any difficulties. We are always ready to help.
    **a.** hesitate     **b.** delay     **c.** stop     **d.** expect

# 64 Confusing words – 3

It doesn't matter if you make mistakes when you're using English — that's how you learn. However, it does matter if you keep on making the same mistakes. Look back at the exercises in this book which you have found difficult. Are you sure you know how to use the words correctly now? If not, write sentences using the words you aren't sure about.

Choose the correct alternative from each pair.

## Set 1

The controversial issue of whether to bring back capital punishment is **1. currently/presently** in the news again. I **2. wander/wonder** what your **3. attitude/opinion** to the idea of restoring the death **4. penalty/sentence** is? Personally, I'm in two minds; on the one hand, it can be **5. argued/discussed** that it acts as a deterrent to **6. potent/potential** criminals; on the other, there is the fact that most crimes are not premeditated. Criminals **7. incline/tend** to act in the heat of the **8. minute/moment** without considering the possible consequences of their actions. Even if you believe we have the **9. right/rite** to decide who should live or who should **10. die/dye**, would you be prepared to carry out such a sentence? It is surely hypocritical to **11. maintain/support** such measures unless you would be willing to carry out the sentence yourself. In the United Kingdom criminals convicted of murder used to be **12. hanged/hung**, whereas in the States they use the **13. electric/electrical** chair. Nowadays, both of these seem barbaric. Some people have suggested more **14. human/humane** methods of execution. For myself, I do not find any method acceptable. We must find better ways of solving our problems than that!

## Set 2

All the research that has been carried out proves beyond any **1. shade/shadow** of doubt that smoking can seriously **2. damage/hurt** your health. Not only can it lead to cancer, it can also result in heart **3. disease/illness**. The only **4. sensible/sensitive** course of **5. action/activity** is to give it up. What surprises me is the hypocritical attitude that some people **6. adapt/adopt** towards the problem. It's quite common, for example, to come across converts to vegetarianism who **7. insist/persist** in smoking like chimneys. A similar example is the chain-smoking teetotaller. I've tried to **8. brake/break** the habit on a number of **9. events/occasions** but unfortunately all my efforts so far have been in **10. vain/vein**.

# 65 Linking ideas

As your English gets better you will want to express more complicated ideas and to link these ideas together. When you are reading or listening to English notice the words and phrases that are used to do this linking. Make a note of them and use them in sentences to help you to remember them.

**A.** Link the first part of the sentence on the left with the second part on the right. Use one of the following to link the two parts. Use each word or phrase once only.

| although | if | since | so that |
|----------|-----|-------|---------|
| because | in case | so | unless |

1. Take a map with you      a......... he left.
2. The play was very boring      b......... he hated heights.
3. I couldn't unlock it      c......... you pay her more.
4. He agreed to go climbing      d......... it's raining heavily.
5. He got a new alarm clock      e......... they walked out.
6. He hasn't written to us      f......... I had the wrong key.
7. She'll only do the job      g......... you lose your way.
8. I never take an umbrella      h......... he'd get up on time.

Write your answers here:

| 1 | 2 | 3 | 4 | 5 | 6 | 7 | 8 |
|---|---|---|---|---|---|---|---|
| g | e | f | b | h | a | c | d |

Can you write your own sentences using the linking words?

**B.** Match the sentence on the left with the sentence on the right which follows it. Use each sentence once only. Underline the linking words after you have finished.

1. He has to take photos of the places he visits.
2. Not everybody thinks the building is ugly.

a. Meanwhile, they were still sleeping peacefully.
b. On the other hand, we could wait until tomorrow.

3. He thought the talk was fascinating.
4. The smoke started coming up the stairs.
5. Business has been very bad this year.
6. We could ask him now.

c. On the contrary, some people say it looks marvellous.
d. As a result, we have had to close one of our factories.
e. In addition, he's writing a report of his journey.
f. His friend, however, fell asleep halfway through it.

Write your answers here:

in

| 1 | 2 | 3 | 4 | 5 | 6 |
|---|---|---|---|---|---|
| e | c | f | a | d | b |

Can you write pairs of sentences using the linking words?

**C.** Fill in the spaces with the linking words listed below:

**As, as well, but, by that time, however, more than, not just, or, regardless of, such as, therefore, unless, when, whether, which**

Stress is one of the main reasons why heart disease now kills 80,000 women a year — 1. *more than* cancer 2. *or* any other disease. Women will be shocked 3. *when* they read this 4. *as* they're conditioned to think it's mainly a male problem. It's a growing danger 5. *which* affects 6. *not just* high-flying female executives 7. *but* housewives and secretaries 8. *as well*. Heredity — 9. *whether* your parents or grandparents suffered from heart disease — is an important factor. 10. *however*, smoking, poor diet and not enough exercise hugely contribute 11. *regardless* your sex. Women display different symptoms of heart disease and 12. *therefore* may be wrongly diagnosed. Extra tests 13. *such as* electrocardiograms are rarely given 14. *unless* suspicious symptoms seem to warrant it. 15. *By that time*, it may be too late.

81

# 66 Avoiding the issue

Answering people's questions is one thing. Sometimes, however, you either can't or, for some reason, don't want to answer. Complete the following answers. All of them mean 'I can't say' or 'I won't say'. The first letter is given.

1. "Do you think he'll get over his illness?"
   "It's too e . . realy . . . to say."

2. "Are you going to apply for the job or not?"
   "It d . . . . . . . . . . . I'll have to think about it."

3. "Are you sure you'll like it in Australia?"
   "I don't know r . . . . . . . . ."

4. "Do you think you did OK in the exam?"
   "It's d . . . . . . . . to say."

5. "Do you think she likes you?"
   "It's h . . . . . . . . to tell with her."

6. "Are you going to tell them?"
   "I'm not s . . . . . . . . yet."

7. "Did what they said upset you?"
   "I'd r . . . . . . . . not say."

8. "Don't you think you're being a bit over-sensitive?"
   "How do you m . . . . . . . . ?"

9. "Where are my glasses?"
   "I"ve no i . . . . . . . . ."

10. "Do you think your boss will give me an interview?"
    "It's not f . . . . . . . . me to say."

11. "Why didn't they phone us this morning?"
    "Don't a . . . . . . . . me."

12. "Do you happen to know the dollar exchange rate?"
    "S . . . . . . . . me."

The next three examples are in more sensitive situations:

13. "Are they having an affair?"
    "I r . . . . . . . . don't think it's got anything to do with us."

14. "How much does he earn?"
    "I'm afraid that's c . . . . . . . . information."

15. "So is she going to lose her job?"
    "I'm not really in a p . . . . . . . . to say."

# 67 Word partnerships – 4

You have seen in previous exercises that words are often used together to form word partnerships. Take some common nouns and see how many adjectives you can think of to go in front of them. You will find that some adjectives can go with many nouns while others have a more restricted use.

From the list below choose adjectives that can form common word partnerships with each of the nouns. In some cases an adjective can go with more than one noun. You do not have to fill every space provided.

| | | | |
|---|---|---|---|
| bumpy | fast | main | sports |
| busy | fizzy | noisy | strong |
| comfortable | foam | non-alcoholic | vintage |
| cool | inflatable | soft | winding |

car

1................
................
................
................
................

cushion

2................
................
................
................
................

drink

3................
................
................
................
................

road

4................
................
................
................
................

# 68 Word formation – 4

When you look up a word in a dictionary, see if any other words can be formed from it.

Sometimes you find these extra words with the definition of the original word and sometimes they have their own definition. This means that it is a good idea to check the words before and after every new word you look up.

Some adjectives can be formed by adding **-ful, -ly** or **-y** to a noun. Sometimes changes in spelling are necessary, for example:

beauty    beaut**iful**    life    li**vely**    noise    noi**sy**

Complete each sentence with an adjective formed from the noun in brackets.

1.  You must be . . . . . . . . when you open the door. (CARE) *careful*
2.  The countryside looks very . . . . . . . . now. (COLOUR) *colourful*
3.  That was a very . . . . . . . . thing to do! (COWARD) *cowardly*
4.  He has a . . . . . . . . routine of exercises. (DAY) *daily*
5.  She was . . . . . . . . when I told her my plan. (DOUBT) *doubtful*
6.  It was very . . . . . . . . so I drove slowly. (FOG) *foggy*
7.  It's nice meeting such a . . . . . . . . person. (FRIEND) *friendly*
8.  He looked very . . . . . . . . in that hat. (FUN) *funny*
9.  They saw a . . . . . . . . figure at the castle door. (GHOST) *ghostly*
10. Working on the car made her hands . . . . . . . . . (GREASE) *greasy*
11. Let's go for a . . . . . . . . walk in the fresh air! (HEALTH) *healthy*
12. We're . . . . . . . . that they'll agree to come. (HOPE) *hopeful*
13. Seeing all that food made me very . . . . . . . . (HUNGER) *hungry*
14. She married a . . . . . . . . businessman. (SUCCESS) *successful*
15. He looked . . . . . . . . when he heard the news. (THOUGHT) *thoughtful*
16. You can trust her. She's a very . . . . . . . . girl. (TRUTH) *truthful*
17. This map was very . . . . . . . . on my holiday. (USE) *useful*
18. It was . . . . . . . . to see him again. (WONDER) *wonderful*

84

# 69 Hotel symbols

If you ever go on holiday in an English-speaking country, you can get a lot of vocabulary from the information about hotels and places to visit. If you stay at an international hotel in your country you may also find information in English but be careful some of this information is not always in the best English!

Below you will see some symbols with explanations. Some words are missing. Put in the missing words by choosing from the following list. Use each word once only.

| accepted | coffee | electric | ground |
| arrangement | cots | entertainment | indoor |
| available | disabled | games | proprietor |
| central | discounts | garage | welcomes |

Hotel 1. _welcomes_ children and has special facilities for them e.g. 2. _cots_ , high chairs etc.

Tea and 3. _coffee_ -making facilities in every room.

GE  Gas/4. _electric_ fires in bedrooms.

PD  Pensioners' low season 5. _discount_ .

6. _central_ heating.

Dogs 7. _accepted_ by arrangement.

Special facilities for 8. _disable_ Check with

9. _proprietor_

D  Diet by 10. _arrangement_ .

Evening 11. _entertainment_ at least once a week in summer.

12. _ground_ floor bedrooms.

Parking/13. _garage_ facilities.

14. _indoor_ swimming pool.

Garden 15. _available_ for guests' use.

Recreation/16. _games_ room.

# 70 Science and technology

Choose the best alternative to complete the sentence.
Look up any words you don't know.

1. The magnet . . . . . . . . . the piece of metal.
   a. attacked    b. attached    c. erupted    **d. attracted**

2. There are many satellites in . . . . . . . . around the earth.
   a. circle    **b. orbit**    c. circumference   d. launch

3. As the car came down the hill, the brakes . . . . . . . . . and it crashed into a wall.
   a. fell    b. broke    c. cracked    **d. failed**

4. The air we breathe mainly consists . . . . . . . . oxygen and nitrogen.
   **a. of**    b. in    c. off    d. with

5. When you heat this metal rod it . . . . . . . . .
   a. contracts    b. expires    c. fills    **d. expands**

6. An electric . . . . . . . . . flowed through the wire.
   a. currant    **b. current**    c. cover    d. wave

7. The water soon . . . . . . . . . in the heat.
   a. melted    b. dissolved    **c. evaporated**   d. froze

8. Some things, paper for example, . . . . . . . . . fire very easily.
   **a. catch**    b. take    c. reach    d. get

9. To receive satellite T.V. you need a special . . . . . . . . .
   a. area    **b. aerial**    c. reception    d. screen

10. For this type of photography you need an extremely . . . . . . . . light-meter.
    a. sensible    b. sensual    c. sensational   **d. sensitive**

11. Stir the salt in the warm water until it . . . . . . . . .
    a. melts    **b. dissolves**    c. breaks    d. digests

12. Radar . . . . . . . . . pilots to land in difficult weather conditions.
    a. lets    **b. enables**    c. succeeds    d. makes

13. The leaves were . . . . . . . . . up a long tube into the machine.
    **a. sucked**    b. sipped    c. slipped    d. slid

14. This plane can fly at over twice the speed of . . . . . . . . .
    **a. sound**    b. flight    c. noise    d. bang

# Test 1 Units 1-14

Choose the best alternative to complete the sentence.

1. If you don't know what a word means, look it . . up . . . . . . .
   a. after        b. down        c. in        **d.** up

2. I'm afraid I can't come tonight. – Oh dear. what a pity . . . .
   a. So do I        b. What luck        **c.** What a pity        d. What do you do

3. The doctor . prescribed . . some different medicine this time.
   a. advised        **b.** prescribed        c. resigned        d. subscribed

4. There were over 50 . . . . . . . . . for the job as caretaker.
   **a.** applicants        b. consumers        c. employers        d. undertakers

5. Oh no! The . . . . . . . . . is broken! How can we open the bottle now?
   a. cracker        **b.** corkscrew        c. key        d. screwdriver

6. Pete's so moody these days. What's come . . . . . . . . . him?
   a. along        **b.** on        c. off        **d.** over

7. Sally couldn't pay the rent so she was . . . . . . . . . from her flat.
   a. disallowed        **b.** evicted        c. prevented        d. prohibited

8. We weren't very hungry so we just had a . . . . . . . . . snack.
   a. faint        b. heavy        **c.** light        d. slight

9. The water is . . . . . . . . . enough for us to drive through the stream.
   a. deep        b. hollow        c. little        **d.** shallow

10. The document you want should be in that filing . . . . . . . . . .
    **a.** cabinet        **b.** case        c. cupboard        d. drawer

11. I'm afraid I threw your letter into the . . . . . . . . . paper bin.
    a. litter        b. rubbish        c. spare        **d.** waste

12. Please don't wear green! It just doesn't . . . . . . . . . you!
    a. fit        **b.** go with        c. make        **d.** suit

13. I'm sure we're all very . . . . . . . . . in what you have to say.
    a. delighted        b. delightful        **c.** interested        d. interesting

14. That cup is very full. Try not to . . . . . . . . . your coffee.
    a. drop        b. fall        c. spare        **d.** spill

15. You must have a . . . . . . . . . diet if you want to stay healthy.
    **a.** balanced        b. even        c. measured        d. relaxed

87

# Test 2 Units 15–28

Choose the best alternative to complete the sentence.

1. Will we ever . . . . . . . . . the truth about the accident?
   **a.** break into     **b.** carry out     **c.** find out     **d.** go with

2. What's your favourite kind of fish? – . . . . . . . . . . , I think.
   **a.** chop     **b.** cutlet     **c.** trout     **d.** veal

3. Simon . . . . . . . . . her offer of a job as the salary was too low.
   **a.** accepted     **b.** failed     **c.** rejected     **d.** released

4. Good  news! Our sales have . . . . . . . . . by 50%!
   **a.** decreased     **b.** increased     **c.** lengthened     **d.** raised

5. I'll leave you to . . . . . . . . . yourself to the vegetables.
   **a.** feed     **b.** help     **c.** serve     **d.** trust

6. You've got a great . . . . . . . . . from up here, haven't you.
   **a.** look     **b.** sight     **c.** sightseeing     **d.** view

7. During the storm the tree was . struck . . . by lightning.
   **a.** beaten     **b.** blown down     **c.** stuck     **d.** struck

8. A few flakes of . . . . . . . . . fell from the sky.
   **a.** frost     **b.** mist     **c.** rain     **d.** snow

9. My watch has stopped. What time do you . . . . . . . . . it?
   **a.** do     **b.** make     **c.** note     **d.** show

10. Why does Kathy make such a . . . . . . . . . of her nephew?
    **a.** favour     **b.** fuss     **c.** kindness     **d.** pride

11. What do you do for a . . . . . . . . . ? – I'm a plumber.
    **a.** course     **b.** life     **c.** living     **d.** salary

12. Most workers here belong to a . . . . . . . . . union.
    **a.** business     **b.** commerce     **c.** job     **d.** trade

13. If you'll . . . . . . . . . me, I must just go and say hello to someone.
    **a.** accuse     **b.** defuse     **c.** excuse     **d.** refuse

14. Thanks for everything. – Not at all. It's been a . . . . . . . . . .
    **a.** kindness     **b.** gratitude     **c.** pleasure     **d.** treasure

15. Oh my back! I think I've . . . . . . . . . a muscle.
    **a.** blistered     **b.** broken     **c.** pulled     **d.** stained

# Test 3 Units 29–43

Choose the best alternative to complete the sentence.

1. I see bus . . . . . . . . . . are going up again next week.
   **a.** fares **b.** fees **c.** incomes **d.** premiums

2. Is it all right if I pay . . . . . . . . . . cheque?
   **a.** by **b.** in **c.** on **d.** with

3. We will only change goods if you have a . . . . . . . . . . .
   **a.** charge **b.** recipe **c.** receipt **d.** slip

4. Is this really . . . . . . . . . . to our discussion?
   **a.** actual **b.** current **c.** registered **d.** relevant

5. I wouldn't spend so much on a new dress. I'm not that . . . . . . . . . . !
   **a.** costly **b.** expensive **c.** extravagant **d.** reluctant

6. What have you been . . . . . . . . . . ? –Oh nothing much. The usual things.
   **a.** about **b.** down to **c.** out with **d.** up to

7. Tony was disqualified . . . . . . . . . . the championships for taking drugs.
   **a.** for **b.** from **c.** of **d.** out of

8. The new theme park is our most popular tourist . . . . . . . . . . .
   **a.** admiration **b.** attraction **c.** pleasure **d.** treasure

9. Why are you limping? – I've . . . . . . . . . . my ankle.
   **a.** bent **b.** folded **c.** sprained **d.** torn

10. Can I use some of this paper to . . . . . . . . . . the present in?
    **a.** lick **b.** stick **c.** stamp **d.** wrap

11. We've moved to that new . . . . . . . . . . of flats near the town centre.
    **a.** block **b.** building **c.** height **d.** tower

12. May I ask a question? – Of course. . . . . . . . . . . .
    **a.** Go ahead **b.** Go off **c.** Take off **d.** Take on

13. Do you think this blouse . . . . . . . . . . my skirt?
    **a.** goes on **b.** goes with **c.** takes after **d.** takes out

14. This bread is . . . . . . . . . . How long ago did you buy it?
    **a.** rough **b.** stale **c.** strong **d.** weak

15. An old man with . . . . . . . . . . clothes wandered into the shop.
    **a.** broken **b.** cramped **c.** shabby **d.** shifty

89

# Test 4 Units 44–57

Use the correct alternative to complete the sentence.

1. This tea isn't sweet enought! – Have you . . . . . . . . . . it?
   **a.** blown      **b.** steered      **c.** stirred      **d.** trialled

2. We . . . . . . . . . from the hotel early the following morning.
   **a.** called off      **b.** passed out      **c.** set off      **d.** turned off

3. James hates being dependent . . . . . . . . . . his parents for money.
   **a.** for      **b.** of      **c.** on      **d.** to

4. Mary's new car is smaller and much more . . . . . . . . . . on petrol.
   **a.** cheap      **b.** economic      **c.** economical      **d.** less

5. Don't bother to ask him for money. It would be a . . . . . . . . . of time.
   **a.** want      **b.** loss      **c.** refusal      **d.** waste

6. You have to pay a . . . . . . . . . . of 100 dollars to reserve your holiday.
   **a.** caution      **b.** deposit      **c.** receipt      **d.** fine

7. The policeman gave Ann first . . . . . . . . . . until the ambulance arrived.
   **a.** aid      **b.** assistance      **c.** emergency      **d.** help

8. Our new shampoo gets rid of . . . . . . . . . – FAST!
   **a.** baldness      **b.** dandruff      **c.** partings      **d.** spots

9. The play was so boring that we left during the . . . . . . . . . . .
   **a.** breakdown      **b.** interval      **c.** pause      **d.** stop

10. Our . . . . . . . . . agent managed to sell the house quite quickly.
    **a.** accommodation      **b.** building      **c.** estate      **d.** state

11. Students must . . . . . . . . . for these courses by the end of the week.
    **a.** enrol      **b.** propose      **c.** subscribe      **d.** write down

12. I hear you didn't get very good . . . . . . . . . . in your exam.
    **a.** additions      **b.** crosses      **c.** marks      **d.** ticks

13. Why doesn't he settle down and get a . . . . . . . . . . job?
    **a.** fixed      **b.** stable      **c.** steady      **d.** sure

14. I'm not in the . . . . . . . . . of borrowing money from friends.
    **a.** custom      **b.** habit      **c.** tradition      **d.** way

15. This room is . . . . . . . . . . ! Doesn't it ever get cleaned?
    **a.** faulty      **b.** filthy      **c.** hideous      **d.** spotless

# Test 5 Units 58–70

Choose the best answer to complete the sentence.

1. I'd like to apologise . . . . . . . . . . being late this morning.
   **a.** at      **b.** for      **c.** of      **d.** to

2. Instead of getting angry, John just . . . . . . . . . his shoulders.
   **a.** shook      **b.** shrugged      **c.** slapped      **d.** twisted

3. Mr Daws handed the . . . . . . . . . of the company over to his daughter.
   **a.** employment      **b.** management      **c.** operating      **d.** undertaking

4. Sally . . . . . . . . blames someone else if things ever go wrong.
   **a.** incompetently    **b.** inconsiderably    **c.** indifferently    **d.** invariably

5. Several employees threatened to . . . . . . . . . unless conditions improved.
   **a.** dismiss      **b.** miss      **c.** resign      **d.** sack

6. I intend to . . . . . . . . . new proposals at the next meeting.
   **a.** make out      **b.** put forward      **c.** put on      **d.** set off

7. These people . . . . . . . . . in claiming that the earth is flat!
   **a.** consist      **b.** insist      **c.** persist      **d.** resist

8. I shouldn't have shouted. I acted in the heat of the . . . . . . . . . .
   **a.** fire      **b.** minute      **c.** moment      **d.** second

9. You'd better take an umbrella . . . . . . . . . it rains later.
   **a.** because      **b.** in case      **c.** since      **d.** so that

10. Where does he live? – I'm afraid that's . . . . . . . . . information.
    **a.** confident      **b.** confidential      **c.** searching      **d.** secretive

11. We are not really in a . . . . . . . . . to give you any definite information.
    **a.** point      **b.** position      **c.** stage      **d.** way

12. His wife discovered he was having a(n) . . . . . . . . . with his secretary.
    **a.** affair      **b.** business      **c.** incident      **d.** love

13. The hotel has tea and coffee-making . . . . . . . . . in every room.
    **a.** availability      **b.** facilities      **c.** occasions      **d.** preparations

14. The baby was sound asleep in her . . . . . . . . . .
    **a.** cot      **b.** couch      **c.** settee      **d.** sofa

15. . . . . . . . . . this powder in half a glass of water and take twice a day.
    **a.** Break      **b.** Dissolve      **c.** Resolve      **d.** Thaw

# Answers

**1** 1.petal 2.fail an examination, knit a sweater, lick a stamp, obey an order, tell a joke 3.up, out, after, for 4.originality, original, originally 5.sew, cough, sweat, height, lost 6.com**plete**, cor**rect**, **dic**tionary, expla**na**tion, **or**igin, or**ig**inal, origi**nal**ity, o**rig**inally, **ped**al, to**geth**er, under**stand**, vo**cab**ulary

**2** 1.elephant, giraffe, lion, monkey 2.accelerator, brake, tyre, windscreen 3.goal, referee, score, team 4.dig, flowers, hedge, plant 5.brooch, earring, necklace, ring 6.platform, return, single, station

**3** 1.i 2.l 3.b 4.a 5.h 6.j 7.c 8.k 9.d 10.f 11.g 12.e

**4** Set 1 1.c 2.i 3.a 4.h 5.f 6.d 7.e 8.j 9.b 10.g Set 2 1.b 2.c 3.e 4.a 5.j 6.h 7.f 8.i 9.d 10.g

**5** 1.a 2.o 3.l 4.e 5.d 6.i 7.r 8.m 9.q 10.n 11.p 12.k 13.b 14.j 15.f 16.c 17.h 18.g

**6** 1.c 2.b 3.d 4.b 5.d 6.c 7.a 8.b 9.a 10.d 11.c 12.b

**7** 1.top hat 2.train 3.teddy bear 4.comb 5.cassette 6.dollar bill 7.cup and saucer 8.newspaper 9.postcard 10.suitcase 11.alarm clock 12.camera 13.banana 14.toothbrush 15.ambulance 16.lighter 17.key 18.parcel 19.shoe 20.corkscrew

**8** 1.Come out 2.came across 3.Come along 4.came off 5.come over 6.come from 7.came up 8.come undone 9.get on 10.getting tired 11.got up 12.getting ... ready 13.get over 14.got into 15.Get off 16.got used

**9** 1 Across 1.proof 4.ideal 5.taste Down 1.print 2.opens 3.false 2 Across 1.Waste 4.evict 5.eager Down 1.Where 2.sting 3.enter

**10** 1.present 2.professional 3.sharp 4.shallow 5.cool 6.light 7.tight 8.high 9.generous 10.public 11.smooth 12.alcoholic 13.sensible 14.permanent 15.thick 16.strong

**11** 1.clock 2.filing cabinet 3.computer 4.rubber 5.telephone 6.briefcase 7.waste paper bin 8.pad 9.pencil 10.ruler 11.calculator 12.chair 13.scissors 14.tray 15.files 16.plant 17.calendar 18.desk

**12** 1.alone 2.between 3.sleepy 4.borrow 5.delighted 6.for 7.interested 8.job 9.journey 10.homework 11.lay 12.suit 13.notice 14.quite 15.reminds 16.robbed 17.stop 18.whose

**13** 1.rural 2.hotel 3.final 4.awful 5.local 6.equal 7.spill 8.smell 9.label

**14** Set 1 1.f 2.c 3.i 4.g 5.h 6.b 7.d 8.a 9.e 10.j Set 2 1.h 2.f 3.i 4.d 5.j 6.g 7.c 8.e 9.b 10.a

**15** 1.chair, back 2.broom, handle 3.butterfly, wing 4.kangaroo, ears 5. baby buggy, wheel 6.television, switches 7.violin, strings 8.crane, hook 9.bike, handlebars

**16** 5.j 6.a 2.c 9.e 4.i 1.h 8.f 10.g 3.b 7.d 1.go with 2.find out 3.carry on turning up 4.call off 5.came across 6.broke into 7.join in 8.passed away 9.get over

**17** 1.soup 2.medium 3.roast beef 4.lamb chop 5.meat 6.fish 7.trout 8.carrots 9.chips 10.desserts 11. peach 12.vanilla 13.white 14.tea 15.alcoholic 16.red

**18** 1.reject 2.lend 3.fill 4.pass 5.miss 6.export 7.decrease 8.cry 9.win 10.hate 11.shut 12.forget 13.set 14.receive 15.lengthen 16.end

**19** 1.cabd 2.dacb 3.dbca 4.acbd 5.cadb 6.acbd 7.bdac

**20** 1.cabin 2.course 3.head 4.note 5.block 6.service 7.spot 8.shade 9.bank 10.ring 11.trunk 12.present 13.tank 14.star 15.tap 16.change

**21** 1.briefcase 2.clock 3.tyre pump 4.cosmetic set 5.video recorder 6.kitchen scales 7.handbag 8.television 9.hair drier 10.frying pan 11.sunglasses 12.film 13. rug 14.tent 15.pen 16.electric heater

**22** 1.c 2.c 3.b 4.c 5.d 6.d 7.a 8.b 9.d 10.d 11.a 12.d 13.c 14.a 15.d

**23** 1.town 2.price 3.bear 4.mood 5.lose 6.niece 7.sew 8.said 9.cost 10.foot 11.does 12.on 13.here 14.home 15.too 16.height 17.lord 18.horse

**24** 1.do 2.made 3.to make 4.done 5.do 6.to make 7.made 8.do 9.make 10.done 11.do 12.do 13.does 14.making 15.make 16.make 17.do 18.make 19.do 20.made 21.make 22.done 23.made 24.doing 25.made 26.do 27.make 28.do 29.do 30.make 31.make 32.make

**25** 1.k 2.n 3.m 4.o 5.a 6.c 7.f 8.e 9.i 10.j 11.b 12.l 13.d 14.p 15.g 16.h

**26** 1.dacb 2.cbda 3.cadb 4.dbac 5.cbad 6.adcb

**27** 1.conductor 2.guitarist 3.juggler 4.ballet dancer 5.clown 6.ventriloquist 7.drummer 8.magician 9.DJ 10.audience 11.cinema 12.orchestra 13.balcony 14.spotlight 15.joke 16.announcer 17.rehearsal 18.critic 19.studio 20.scriptwriter 21.understudy 22.interval 23.opera 24.row 25.scene 26.string 27.tune 28.LP

**28** 1.c 2.a 3.b 4.b 5.d 6.c 7.a 8.c 9.c 10.b 11.d 12.d 13.a 14.c 15.c 16.b

**29** 1.EDUCATION 2.FURNITURE 3.ACCOMMODATION 4.MEDICAL 5.HOLIDAYS & TRAVEL 6.CLAIRVOYANTS 7.BOATS 8.BABY & NURSERY 9.GARDENING 10.PERSONAL 11.MUSICAL 12.PHOTOGRAPHY

**30** 1.b 2.d 3.a 4.b 5.c 6.a 7.c 8.b 9.d 10.a 11.c 12.a 13.b 14.a 15.c 16.c

**31** 1.elephant, trunk 2.rhinoceros, horn 3.ostrich, feathers 4.parrot, beak 5.squirrel, tail 6.tortoise, shell 7.crab, claw 8.horse, hoof 9.bear, paw

**32** 1.relevant 2.confident 3.independent 4.patient 5.disobedient 6.pleasant 7.absent 8.permanent 9.observant 10.important 11.current 12.extravagant 13.reluctant 14.incompetent 15.convenient

**33** 1.bdac 2.dbac 3.adcb 4.cadb 5.cadb 6.bdac

**34** 1.Ingredients 2.sift 3.bowl 4.Pour 5.break 6.Stir 7.rest 8.beat 9.Melt 10.batter 11.stick 12.turn 13.keep 14.Serve

**35** 1.i 2.e 3.g 4.h 5.a 6.d 7.b 8.c 9.l 10.f 11.j 12.k

**36** 1.b 2.d 3.a 4.b 5.c 6.b 7.a 8.c 9.b 10.b 11.d 12.c 13.d 14.a 15.c 16.d

**37** 1.saw 2.hammer 3.chisel 4.pliers 5.ruler 6.plane 7.drill 8.screwdriver 9.spanner 10.paint brush 11.axe 12.file 1.hammer 2.axe 3.spanner 4.pliers 5.file

**38** 1.action, activity, inactive, actress 2.additives, addition 3.admirable, admiration 4.disadvantage, advantageous 5.advertising, advertisement 6.disagree, agreement 7.attractions, attractively 8.basic, basis 9.calculations, calculator, calculating 10.collecting, collectors, collection 11.comparison, comparatively, comparable 12.competitors, competitive, competition 13.confirmation, unconfirmed 14.continuation, discontinued continually, continuous

**39** Set 1 1.a 2.j 3.d 4.i 5.e 6.c 7.b 8.f 9.h 10.g Set 2 1.j 2.i 3.f 4.d 5.g 6.b 7.a 8.h 9.e 10.c

**40** 1.d 2.e 3.k 4.b 5.j 6.i 7.l 8.a 9.h 10.c 11.f 12.g

**41** 1.go grey 2.goes/went on 3.went out 4.went off 5.goes/went ... with 6.go ahead 7.gone up 8.go together 9.take place 10.took ... back 11.Take ... medicine 12.takes after 13.took off 14.take ... out 15.took over 16.take ... seriously 17.take ... chance 18.Take ... time

**42** 1.exact 2.rough 3.partial 4.stale 5.minor 6.strong 7.shabby 8.positive 9.even 10.artificial 11.considerable 12.hollow 13.flexible 14.faint 15.tough 16.compulsory

**43** Set 1 unavoidable accident, irresponsible behaviour, uncomfortable chair, inedible food, unfavourable report Set 2 unbreakable china, irreversible decision, unreadable novel, unseasonable weather, unreliable witness Set 3 inflexible attitude, improbable explanation, indigestible food, illegible handwriting, incurable illness

**44** 1.g 2.k 3.m 4.a 5.l 6.i 7.e 8.f 9.c 10.n 11.b 12.o 13.h 14.d 15.j

**45** 1.library 2.spoon 3.petrol 4.money 5.dictionary 6.table 7.glasses 8.nose 9.questions 10.whistle 11.egg 12.fly 13.scissors 14.order 15.thick 16.mistakes

**46** 6.c 7.i 2.a 9.h 8.g 1.b 5.d 10.f 3.e 4.j 1.get by 2.going through 3.take after 4.slip up 5.turned ... down 6.put out 7.carry on 8.setting off 9.run away 10.look into

**47** 1.convenient, conveniently, inconvenient 2.creation, creature, creator 3.criticise/ize, criticism, critical 4.decision, indecisive 5.decorator, decorations 6.demonstrators, demonstration 7.dependent, independence 8.dictation, dictatorial 9.direction, directly, directory, directors 10.economical, economics, economically, economise/ize 11.electrician, electricity, electrical, electrical 12.employees, unemployed, employer, employment 13.enthusiastically, enthusiastic

**48** 1.b 2.c 3.a 4.d 5.a 6.b 7.a 8.a 9.c 10.c 11.d 12.a 13.b 14.d 15.a 16.a

**49** 1.nice 2.time 3.mind 4.shame 5.fair 6.silly 7.point 8.surprise 9.same 10.never 11.waste 12.first 13.admit 14.rather

**50** 1.b 2.c 3.b 4.d 5.b 6.b 7.a 8.c 9.a 10.d 11.c 12.c 13.a 14.c 15.a 16.d

**51** 1.n 2.j 3.d 4.f 5.e 6.k 7.c 8.b 9.o 10.p 11.i 12.h 13.a 14.m 15.l 16.g

**52** 1.f 2.l 3.g 4.a 5.b 6.i 7.j 8.k 9.d 10.c 11.e 12.h

**53** 1.g 2.i 3.d 4.a 5.o 6.k 7.b 8.h 9.n 10.f 11.j 12.c 13.e 14.l 15.m

**54** 1.advertise, bachelor, character, sensible 2.assistant, departure, discussion, expensive 3.disagree, lemonade, mispronounce, unemployed 4.advertising, indicator, operator, understatement 5.advertisement, biography, disqualify, receptionist 6.disagreement, indication, operation, understanding

**55** 1.principal 2.staff 3.examination 4.syllabus 5.attend 6.gymnasium 7.mark 8.homework 9.enrol 10.term 11.timetable 12.subject 13.uniform 14.pupil 15.playground

**56** Set 1 1.said 2.raised 3.lose 4.living 5.almost 6.salary 7.missed 8.told 9.arose 10.steady 11.habit 12.later 13.job 14.present 15.economic 16.climate 17.older 18.pays Set 2 1.flair 2.waste 3.opportunity 4.As long 5.However 6.raise 7.make 8.bear 9.affect 10.spend 11.friends 12.watch

**57** 1.fantastic 2.enormous 3.minute 4.boiling 5.freezing 6.gorgeous 7.hideous 8.spotless 9.filthy 10.fascinating 11.tedious 12.impossible 13.charming 14.delicious 15.disgusting

**58** bank clerk, bus conductor, bus driver, cashier, dentist, dustman, electrician, nurse, plumber, policeman, postman, priest, secretary, traffic warden, window cleaner

**59** Set 1 1.f (computerise/ize) 2.b (emphasise/ize) 3.h (identify) 4.g (memorise/ize) 5.a (modernise/ize) 6.i (purify) 7.d (shorten) 8.e (thicken) 9.c (widen) Set 2 1.e (apologise/ize) 2.g (brighten) 3.a (classify) 4.c (loosen) 5.d (sharpen) 6.b (soften) 7.h (specialise/ize) 8.f (strengthen) 9.i (terrorise/ize)

**60** 1.cry, giggle, groan, hum, mumble, scream, shout, sing, stammer, talk, whisper, whistle 2.bend, climb, creep, hop, jump, lift, shake, shrug, slide, slip, snatch, wander

**61** 1.dishonest, honestly, honesty 2.identification, Unidentified 3.imaginary, imagination 4.industrial, industrious, industrialist, industrialised/ized 5.manager, management, Managing, manageress 6.nationality, nationalised/ized, national 7.observant, observatory, observation 8.satisfactory, satisfaction, dissatisfied 9.scientist, scientific, scientifically 10.shortly, shorten, shortage 11.variable, variety, various, invariably

**62** 1.barbecue 2.iron 3.vacuum cleaner 4.necklace 5.camera 6.clothes line 7.bed 8.tape recorder 9.bathroom heater 10.bedside cabinet 11.suitcase 12.clock 13.kettle 14.food mixer 15.game 16.radio

**63** 1.b 2.c 3.c 4.a 5.c 6.d 7.b 8.a 9.a 10.c 11.c 12.d 13.b 14.a 15.a 16.a

**64** Set 1 1.currently 2.wonder 3.attitude 4.penalty 5.argued 6.potential 7.tend 8.moment 9.right 10.die 11.support 12.hanged 13.electric 14.humane Set 2 1.shadow 2.damage 3.disease 4.sensible 5.action 6.adopt 7.persist 8.break 9.occasions 10.vain

**65** A 1.g (in case) 2.e (so) 3.f (because) 4.b (although) 5.h (so that) 6.a (since) 7.c (if) 8.d (unless) B 1.e (In addition) 2.c (On the contrary) 3.f (however) 4.a (Meanwhile) 5.d (As a result) 6.b (On the other hand) C 1.more than 2.or 3.when 4.as 5.which 6.not just 7.but 8.as well 9.whether 10.However 11.regardless of 12.therefore 13.such as 14.unless 15.By that time

**66** 1.early 2.depends 3.really 4.difficult 5.hard 6.sure 7.rather 8.mean 9.idea 10.for 11.ask 12.search 13.really 14.confidential 15.position

**67** 1.comfortable, fast, noisy, sports, vintage 2.comfortable, foam, inflatable, soft 3.cool, fizzy, non-alcoholic, soft, strong 4.bumpy, busy, fast, main, noisy, winding

**68** 1.careful 2.colourful 3.cowardly 4.daily 5.doubtful 6.foggy 7.friendly 8.funny 9.ghostly 10.greasy 11.healthy 12.hopeful 13.hungry 14.successful 15.thoughtful 16.truthful 17.useful 18.wonderful

**69** 1.welcomes 2.cots 3.coffee 4.electric 5.discounts 6.central 7.accepted 8.disabled 9.proprietor 10.arrangement 11.entertainment 12.ground 13.garage 14.indoor 15.available 16.games

**70** 1.d 2.b 3.d 4.a 5.d 6.b 7.c 8.a 9.b 10.d 11.b 12.b 13.a 14.a

| | | | | | | | | | | | | | | | |
|---|---|---|---|---|---|---|---|---|---|---|---|---|---|---|---|
| **Test 1** | 1.d | 2.c | 3.b | 4.a | 5.b | 6.d | 7.b | 8.c | 9.d | 10.a | 11.d | 12.d | 13.c | 14.d | 15.a |
| **Test 2** | 1.c | 2.c | 3.c | 4.b | 5.b | 6.d | 7.d | 8.d | 9.b | 10.b | 11.c | 12.d | 13.c | 14.c | 15.c |
| **Test 3** | 1.a | 2.a | 3.c | 4.d | 5.c | 6.d | 7.b | 8.b | 9.c | 10.d | 11.a | 12.a | 13.b | 14.b | 15.c |
| **Test 4** | 1.c | 2.c | 3.c | 4.c | 5.d | 6.b | 7.a | 8.b | 9.b | 10.c | 11.a | 12.c | 13.c | 14.b | 15.b |
| **Test 5** | 1.b | 2.b | 3.b | 4.d | 5.c | 6.b | 7.c | 8.c | 9.b | 10.b | 11.b | 12.a | 13.b | 14.a | 15.b |